JEFF SPARROW

FASCISTS AMONG US

online hate and the Christchurch massacre

SCRIBE
Melbourne • London

Scribe Publications
2 John St, Clerkenwell, London, WC1N 2ES, United Kingdom
18–20 Edward St, Brunswick, Victoria 3056, Australia
3754 Pleasant Ave, Suite 100, Minneapolis, Minnesota 55409, USA

First published by Scribe in the UK, Australia, and New Zealand 2019
Published by Scribe in North America 2020

Chapter Four draws on arguments originally made in Jeff Sparrow,
'"When the Burning Moment Breaks": gun control and rage massacres',
Overland Literary Journal, August 2012.

Typeset in 11/14.5 pt Fournier by the publishers

Printed and bound in the UK by CPI Group (UK) Ltd, Croydon CR0 4YY

Scribe Publications is committed to the sustainable use of natural resources
and the use of paper products made responsibly from those resources.

9781912854691 (UK edition)
9781925849677 (Australian edition)
9781950354092 (US edition)
9781925938036 (e-book)

Catalogue records for this book are available from the
National Library of Australia and the British Library

scribepublications.co.uk
scribepublications.com.au
scribepublications.com

For Steph

Contents

Introduction: the need to understand   1

1 'An actual fascist': fascisms old and new   9
2 'Sweep it all up!': the world after 9/11   28
3 'Hail Trump!': fascist memes   45
4 'Screw your optics!': the Christchurch strategy   60
5 'Forests, lakes, mountains, and meadows':
    ecofascism and accelerationism   81
6 'Cobbers': Australia and the fascist milieu   94
Conclusion: hope against hate   113

Acknowledgements   133
Notes   135

Meditate that this came about:
I commend these words to you.
Carve them in your hearts
At home, in the street,
Going to bed, rising;
Repeat them to your children,
Or may your house fall apart,
May illness impede you,
May your children turn their faces from you.

—Primo Levi, *If This Is a Man/The Truce*

INTRODUCTION
THE NEED TO UNDERSTAND

On 14 March 2019, a new post appeared on the 8chan politics board /pol/. 'Well lads,' it read, 'it's time to stop shitposting and time to make a real life effort post. I will carry out and [sic] attack against the invaders, and will even live stream the attack via Facebook.'[1]

The post linked to the Facebook page of a 28-year-old Australian man and a 74-page manifesto entitled 'The Great Replacement'.

'[P]lease do your part by spreading my message, making memes and shitposting as you usually do,' it continued.

At 1.40 pm the next day, a man arrived at the Al Noor Mosque in Christchurch, New Zealand, during Friday prayers.

A worshipper greeted him with, 'Hello, brother' — and the stranger opened fire.

He shot worshippers indiscriminately inside the building, returned to his car for more ammunition, and then came back and shot more people. After about six minutes, he drove to the Linwood Islamic Centre and killed people there. One of the men at prayer wrestled with him, and he fled.

At 2.20 pm, police rammed the gunman's car, pulled him from the vehicle, and placed him under arrest.[2] Fifty people were dead — and another died later from wounds.

In her widely praised response to the massacre, New Zealand Prime Minister Jacinda Ardern pledged never to utter the name of the alleged shooter. The people killed that day — and the scores more left physically or mentally scarred — deserved remembrance, she said, and the man who opened fire on them did not.

In an ideal world, the conversation about the mosque shootings would have begun and ended with Ansi Alibava, who came to New Zealand with her husband to start a new life; with Husna Ahmed, who led women out of the building and then was killed when she returned to save her wheelchair-bound husband, Farid; with Haji-Daoud Nabi, who jumped into the firing line to cover friends; with Sayyad Milne, the 14-year-old slain before he could fulfil his dream of playing professional football; and with the many, many others murdered as they worshipped.[3]

Unfortunately, the bullets that took their lives didn't come out of nowhere.

Recent statistics show right-wing violence on the rise. The Center for International and Strategic Studies reports that terror attacks from far-right perpetrators doubled between 2016 and 2017 in the United States, and grew by 43 per cent in Europe in that same period.[4] Between 2009 and 2018, according to the Anti-Defamation League, extremists from the right caused 73 per cent of US domestic terror deaths, compared to 23 per cent of deaths attributed to Islamists and 3 per cent to left-wing terrorists.[5]

The only reason rightists didn't have a monopoly over the fifty deaths from domestic terrorism in 2018 was that one attacker abandoned white supremacism for radical Islamism prior to committing murder.

The alleged perpetrator of the Christchurch massacre might have entered the mosques by himself but, politically, he was never alone. We know that, after growing up in the regional town of Grafton in New South Wales, the accused man used inherited money to travel through Europe — and on those trips he interacted with far-right organisations in many different countries.

We also know that he was deeply invested in the Australian fascist movement. On a secret blog frequented by activists from the far right, Tom Sewell, a leading fascist activist, acknowledged that the alleged perpetrator 'had been around' the so-called patriot movement since before 2016.

'He was well known,' Sewell explained to his co-thinkers, 'for those in the know.'[6] A future mass murderer was 'well known' to other fascists — and none of them did anything to stop him. While Sewell and other activists distanced themselves from the massacre, some posters on platforms such as 8chan and Gab openly applauded the violence — and others called for more killings.

That's why we must understand the alleged perpetrator's ideas, however repellent they are.

I've chosen to refer to the accused killer as Person X. In part, that's because early readers reacted so strongly to the use of his name, suggesting — on the grounds that Jacinda Ardern articulated — that it diminished his victims. Certainly, many will find a discussion about the hateful doctrines that inspired Person X difficult. It would be wrong to make that process more painful.

In any case, the euphemism serves another purpose, emphasising a key argument of this book. The Christchurch gunman emerged from a fascist subculture in which he'd previously been a minor and anonymous figure. Before he stepped into the limelight to shoot innocent people, no one — outside the milieu of the far right — knew who he was.

The next killer will be the same.

The massacre at the Christchurch mosques was an act of terror, consciously designed, in ways many commentators haven't understood, to inspire further acts of terror. It represented a particular strategic choice for the fascist movement, a decision not to build public organisations but to encourage violence by previously unknown individuals acting in isolation.

Already, Christchurch has inspired imitations in San Diego and El Paso. Almost certainly, there will be others. But we have no way of knowing who will carry them out.

Hence, Person X: the anonymous young man who emerges from the shadows, gun in hand, already committed to an evil ideology.

The fascism of the 1930s revolved around names that were publicly shouted — most obviously, Hitler and Mussolini. Likewise, today, the alt-right has spawned a new breed of celebrity, with racist and nationalistic demagogues building profiles through social and conventional media.

The Person X phenomenon represents something else: a strategy for fascist terrorism, one that seeks to incite angry young men to conduct rage massacres, not to achieve any specific ends so much as to destabilise liberal democracies. This plan will not bring fascism to power. It will, however, result in more deaths.

The use of a pseudonym reminds us that, while Person X might be in jail in New Zealand, he's also out there in the world somewhere, browsing a racist internet forum and counting ammunition.

There is, however, an obvious risk in not using the alleged perpetrator's name.

In JK Rowling's Harry Potter series, the characters refer to He-Who-Must-Not-Be-Named, in a vain attempt to ward off the evil Dark Lord. Their refusal to acknowledge Voldemort merely leaves them ill prepared to meet the threat he poses.

Since the Christchurch murders, some commentators have argued that we should refuse to discuss the ideas that motivated the massacre. In particular, politicians have advised against reading Person X's manifesto. In New Zealand, authorities have made possession or distribution of the tract a crime, with many reputable internet service providers deleting it from their servers.

While no doubt well intentioned, such efforts won't prevent Person X's manifesto from circulating among the readers for whom it was intended. As we will see, the document was never particularly directed to the public. It was, first and foremost, an intervention into a specific fascist subculture — and it remains easily accessible on the platforms where right-wing extremists congregate.

In that sense, it's already being studied by the Person Xs of the future. That's why we need to understand it, too.

While I do not name Person X in this book, I do take his ideas seriously. In particular, I discuss his self-identification as a 'fascist' with respect to the history and practice of fascism in the twentieth century. I argue that in the twenty-first century, the terrain on which fascism operated changed dramatically, with anti-Muslim prejudice providing a politically acceptable alternative to anti-Semitism, and with the internet facilitating a new organisational paradigm.

At the same time, I suggest that the Christchurch massacre emerged from the inability of fascists to translate online propaganda into real-world organisation; that, frustrated by the failure of fascist party-building, Person X turned to terror, seeking to politicise the rage massacres that already fascinated a certain kind of young man.

I explain his commitment to 'accelerationism', a project that aims to intensify social contradictions to breaking point, and show how that informs Person X's so-called ecofascism: a version of environmentalism that exults in the destruction it claims to oppose. And I examine the audience for his message by looking at the Australian fascist groups with which Person X interacted.

Fascism remains a marginal force in the English-speaking world. It is, however, a doctrine that feeds on despair — and this is an era in which political despair abounds.

With his murders, Person X sought to forge a path for other fascists to follow. We need to understand him, because we must stop him.

I

'AN ACTUAL FASCIST'

FASCISMS OLD AND NEW

Person X spent considerable effort spelling out his motivations in 'The Great Replacement', the document to which he linked in his final 8chan post.

In the first section, 'Answering possible questions', he provides a kind of FAQ about his ideas. In the second, he writes short responses to specific constituencies (conservatives, liberals, Christians, etc.) before a third section consisting of 'general thoughts and strategies'. The document also contains poetry and images.

In those 74 pages, Person X makes his philosophy entirely clear.

'Are you a fascist?' he asks himself rhetorically.

'Yes,' he says in response. 'For once, the person that will be called a fascist, is an actual fascist.' He then adds, 'I am sure the journalists will love that.'[1]

As it happened, journalists have, by and large, resisted applying the label to Person X, more often describing him as an 'extremist' or simply a 'gunman'.

Perhaps understandably, many prefer psychological explanations for Person X's actions. They depict him as deranged, and declare that no one could take his writings and political ideas seriously. It is, after all, more comforting to think of a mass murderer as unhinged than as calculating and lucid.

Obviously, anyone who can shoot down innocent men, women, and children while they're praying inhabits a different ethical universe from the rest of us. In that sense, almost by definition, Person X can be judged abnormal.

But that is a moral rather than medical diagnosis. In purely clinical terms, some of the world's worst monsters have been both supremely evil and entirely rational. Few serious historians consider Hitler insane.[2]

We will, no doubt, learn more about Person X's psyche. But, if we leave aside a natural revulsion at his deeds, his document doesn't, despite what many journalists have said, read like the ravings of a madman. Person X might not have had much formal education, but his manifesto expresses — with stark clarity — a distinctive political program.

In the classic British comedy *The Young Ones*, the character Rick — a parody of a gormless leftist

— deploys the word 'fascist' against any authority figure, describing as 'fascist' all politicians, social workers, and critics of his poetry. The American attorney Mike Godwin has noted a similar phenomenon on the internet. His 'Godwin's Law' holds that 'as an online discussion grows longer, the probability of a comparison involving Nazis or Hitler approaches one'.[3]

That's why some analysts claim fascism should only be employed to describe a political phenomenon from the distant past. For them, 'Fascism' (with a capital f) refers only to the political tendency that arose in Italy in the 1920s, with the lowercase 'fascism' applying also to German National Socialism. Because both movements came to an end with the Allied victory in the Second World War, attaching the same label to an isolated individual in the very different circumstances of the twenty-first century can only be anachronistic and absurd.

Person X makes precisely that point. He poses the question of whether he might be described as a 'Nazi', and answers in the negative.

'Actual [N]azis do not exist,' he says. 'They haven't been a political or social force anywhere in the world for more than 60 years.'

But if that is true, it's only true in the narrowest sense. 'National socialism' might have died in a Berlin bunker, but the development throughout the 1920s and the 1930s of parties recognisably similar to the Italian fascists and the German National Socialists (the Falange in Spain, the Ustashe in Croatia, the Arrow Cross in Hungary, and many others) implies a 'generic fascism' — a broader but still meaningful category for a distinctive far-right politics of which Hitler was merely one exponent.

Undeniably, delineating that category poses real problems. In a widely cited definition, the scholar Roger Griffin summarises fascism as a 'palingenetic form of populist ultra-nationalism'.[4] If we leave aside palingenesis (that is, mythological rebirth), the nationalism of fascism means its adherents adopted traditions, ideals, and cultures specific to particular countries. In the 1930s, some fascists declared themselves Christians, some embraced paganism or mysticism, and some remained indifferent or hostile to religion. Umberto Eco thus describes fascism as 'a fuzzy totalitarianism, a collage of different philosophical and political ideas, a beehive of contradictions'.[5]

Furthermore, fascist movements typically changed as they developed. The National Socialist German Workers' Party began as one of many tiny *völkisch* groups recruiting war veterans with an anti-Semitic nationalism. It transformed itself, in conditions of economic and political instability, into a powerful street-fighting movement of the downwardly mobile petty bourgeoisie, and then, after significant internal ructions, came to power with the backing of German heavy industry.

Fascism should, in other words, be understood as process rather than a thing, with its mutability over time making static definitions innately difficult. Nonetheless, some generalisations arise from the period of 'classic fascism'.

Fascism was, at heart, a reactionary movement. In a context of deep economic crisis, fascists valorised hierarchy, the supposedly eternal differences between individuals, between men and women, and between ethnic groups.

'There is no one person equal to any other, not identical twins, not countrymen, not workers within a class group and certainly not those of differing races ...' writes Person X, breaking into capitals to emphasise the point. 'DIVERSITY IS UNEQUAL, HIERARCHIES ARE CERTAIN.'

The fascists of the 1930s organised to defeat, and ultimately to physically eliminate, those who advocated or embodied social equality: the labour movement, socialists, social democrats, immigrants, and other 'traitors'.

In their staunch opposition to equality, egalitarianism, and popular democracy — and their support for militarism, nationalism, and traditional gender roles — fascists belonged unequivocally to the political right. Upon achieving power, fascist movements lost much of their specificity, establishing repressive regimes not so dissimilar to authoritarian states arising from different processes. Person X's description of China as having 'the closest political and social values to my own' makes sense in that light. He does not admire the peasant revolt that brought modern China into existence so much as the modern Chinese state: authoritarian, repressive, and nationalistic.

The fascists of the 1930s differed from traditional conservatives in several important respects. Throughout the nineteenth century, the numerically tiny social elite relied on either state power or mercenaries to quell popular unrest. Fascism, by contrast, built its own organisations to destroy mass social-democratic and communist parties. That meant recruiting from the middle of society rather than merely from the top. Fascists could and did attract the wealthy; they could also appeal to industrial workers, particularly in periods of high unemployment. But in most countries, core fascist support came from the so-called small men: artisans, professionals, shopkeepers, policemen, and individual proprietors of relatively humble means, aghast at being dominated by a working class they saw as beneath them.

In the context of intractable crisis, fascism weaponised middle-class fear, transforming dentists, clerks, and grocers into a formidable paramilitary force. Yet, despite their hostility to unions and socialists, the key recruits to fascism didn't entirely share the agenda of the social elite. The 'small men' felt themselves menaced by big business just as much as by labour unrest. A lawyer or a baker in Weimar Germany might well have feared communist agitation. But he was just as likely to loathe the bankers and businessmen who were prospering during a crisis that threatened his very survival.

That contradiction gave fascism its distinctive duality.

In Italy and in Germany, Mussolini and Hitler eventually formed governments with the support of industrialists who, after considerable hesitation, embraced the fascists as a necessary evil and the only force capable of destroying an insurgent labour movement. Elsewhere, even when fascism wasn't able to take power, its leaders usually recognised the need to forge an eventual alliance with the big end of town.

Yet, even as fascist movements negotiated with elites, they promised their own cadres something entirely different: a new order in which the little man of the city, stunted by the banality of commerce, would be reborn into an authentic, heroic life.

Griffin's one-line gloss emphasises fascism's rhetoric of national regeneration, which typically combined an invocation of a mythical past with an embrace of high technology, modernity, and innovation. In another influential definition, Robert O Paxton explains fascism as:

a form of political behavior marked by obsessive preoccupation with community decline, humiliation, or victimhood, and by compensatory cults of unity, energy, and purity, in which a mass-based party of committed nationalist militants, working in uneasy but effective collaboration with traditional elites, abandons democratic liberties and pursues with redemptive violence and without ethical or legal restraints goals of internal cleansing and external expansion.[6]

Before the Second World War, fascists adopted a variety of methods to square the circle of their commitment to reaction and radicalism. Their organisations depended on authoritarianism to hold together people more accustomed to small-business competition than labour collaboration. A cult around a Man of Destiny allowed fascists to make different promises to different constituencies, with the great leader presenting organisational tacks and turns as manifestations of his mysterious but infallible wisdom.

Fascist racism also facilitated a faux militancy entirely compatible with reaction. Hitlerite anti-Semitism, for instance, buttressed the 'socialist' side of National Socialism, as agitators depicted Jews as financiers, bankers, and speculators oppressing ordinary Germans. Brutality directed at impoverished Jewish men, women, and children could then be described as revolutionary action taken against the secret masters of the world.

But a key element in the fascist project was always violence.

'Fascism,' writes Daniel Woodley, 'is distinguished from liberalism by the aestheticization of struggle and the glorification of paramilitary violence as primary features of political action ... For fascists "creative violence" is contrasted with the insipid cowardice of liberal intellectualism: violence is not just a means to an end, but an *intrinsic value* in itself.'[7]

In *Mein Kampf*, Hitler admired left-wing demonstrations because, he said, they 'burned into the small, wretched individual the proud conviction that, paltry worm as he was, he was nevertheless a part of a great dragon'.[8] But, as I have noted above, the middle-class recruits to fascism lacked the collective traditions of the left. So, instead of the solidarity of the factory, fascists looked to war as a model of excitement, purpose, and fraternity.

Both Mussolini and Hitler recruited heavily — especially at first — from demobilised Great War soldiers, building what Mussolini called 'a trenchocracy of ex-combatants: a new elite that had emerged from a baptism of fire'.[9] Italian fascism emphasised the spirit of *combattentismo* exemplified by veterans, while National Socialism stressed the camaraderie of the Freikorps, military units that transitioned from fighting the Allies in the trenches to battling communists in the streets of Berlin.

'People told us that the War was over,' said the Freikorps leader Friedrich Wilhelm Heinz. 'That made us laugh. We ourselves are the War. Its flame burns strongly in us. It envelopes our whole being, and fascinates us with the enticing urge to destroy'.[10]

The historian George Mosse describes how, across Europe, fascists saw the society that had emerged from the war 'as an enemy which as shock troops they must destroy'.[11]

Crucially, fascist violence didn't simply provide a means through which the promised national rebirth would be achieved. It was, in a sense, itself that rebirth, with combat against the internal foe (the communist, the Jew, the intellectual) the crucible from which a new superman would arise. The reconstitution of society and the reconstitution of the individual were a single project — the consequence of the war the fascist waged against his enemies.

In his manifesto, Person X presents precisely this sentiment: 'Radical, explosive action is the only desired, and required, response to an attempted genocide … [Young men and women] decry weakness, mock fecklessness and worship strength, and in this worship of strength they radicalize and find the solution.'[12]

In another place, he explains, 'the struggle is a beauty in itself, and the victory will be all the sweeter because of it'.[13]

This is the rhetoric of classical fascism.

Yet an obvious gulf exists between mass movements of the 1920s and 1930s and the small coterie of fascist thugs in most developed countries today — or, indeed, an individual murderer like Person X.

The Allied victory in 1945 marked a turning point for the English-speaking world, transforming fascism from a mass phenomenon into (for the most part) a fringe preoccupation.

In what sense, then, can we talk of fascism as persisting after the war? What continuity exists between the past and the present?

Person X nominates Sir Oswald Mosley as 'the person from history closest to my own beliefs' — and because Mosley's career straddled the pre-war and post-war era, he provides an ideal illustration of the evolution of twentieth-century fascism.

Oswald Mosley was born in 1896 into an aristocratic Staffordshire family that blamed its reduced influence on a nefarious modernity. He served, and was injured, in the Royal Flying Corps during the Great War, an experience that bolstered his subsequent association with danger, speed, and technology. Like Mussolini, Hitler, and other fascists from the classic period,

Mosley treasured the camaraderie of his service, particularly in contrast with the factional divisions of civilian life.

He first won a parliamentary seat in 1918 as a Conservative, establishing himself as an orator representing the younger war generation in opposition to the 'old gang' of conventional politicians. He became an independent in 1920, and then, in 1924, joined the Labour Party. With unemployment climbing to 16 per cent by 1930, Mosley outlined his own semi-Keynesian, semi-corporatist program for economic repair — and, upon its rejection by the Labour leadership, resigned his membership.

In 1931, he launched his own New Party, which brought him, for the first time, into conflict with the trade unions. 'That is the crowd that has prevented anyone from doing anything in England since the war,' he complained after being jostled by Labour supporters.[14] Thereafter, the New Party trained young men, often with military experience, as 'Mosley's Biff Boys', eventually creating something like a paramilitary force.

In 1932, the New Party gave way to the British Union of Fascists, an organisation explicitly putting forward an Anglicised interpretation of ideas borrowed from Mussolini and (later) Hitler.

Mosley advocated a radical economic program of national protectionism, implemented by what he called a

'Modern Dictatorship': a version of Mussolini's corporatist state, made feasible by the revitalising will of fascist 'super-men'.

For a period, the BUF seemed poised for a breakthrough. At its peak, it had a membership of about 50,000 people, with its activists often coming from various professional occupations. It briefly enjoyed the support of establishment figures such as the press baron Lord Rothermere, who backed fascism in Britain (as he had in Italy) as a counter to the communism he loathed. Rothermere's *Daily Mail* infamously ran an editorial entitled 'Hurrah for the Blackshirts!'; his *Evening Standard* ran a competition for readers to sum up 'Why I like the Blackshirts' on a postcard.[15]

By 1936, the group styled itself the British Union of Fascists and National Socialists (or simply the British Union). The group founded its own Black House (in imitation of Hitler's Brown House), where its members studied martial arts and performed paramilitary drills. Mosley's supporters wore a blackshirted uniform adorned with a lightning bolt in a circle. They addressed him as 'the Leader', and greeted him with 'Hail Mosley' and the stiff-armed salute.[16]

A poem 'We Follow' from the BU press encapsulated the group's distinctively fascist outlook, celebrating Mosley with almost religious fervour:

We ask no easy path –
Show us a way
That's harder, grander,
Nobler than of old.
Teach us to strive, and
Glory in the strife,
Nor falter when the flame
Of life grows cold;
But meet Death with a Laugh,
not tear or sigh.
We ask thee, Leader,
teach Us how to die![17]

Over time, the BUF became overtly anti-Semitic, with Mosley denouncing the 'big Jews' in business and the 'little Jews' who threatened British identity via immigration.[18]

It also grew increasingly violent. At a notorious meeting at Olympia, Mosley used searchlights to highlight hecklers to be systematically beaten up by his troops. One of the journalists present mused as to why Mosley paused his speech during interjections, even though his powerful loudspeakers could easily have drowned them out. 'Slowly we all understood,' he wrote, 'that it was done to allow his Blackshirts to make a thorough mess of the interrupter …'[19]

The consistent resistance to Mosley from Jewish and socialist groups ultimately led Rothermere and other potential backers to abandon him, judging the BUF as likely to provoke (rather than quell) industrial unrest.

As the conflict in Europe drew closer, Mosley argued for appeasement, declaring 'a million Britons shall never die in your Jews' quarrel'.[20] The BUF campaigned for peace during the so-called Phoney War of 1939 and early 1940, before being banned in the middle of the year. Mosley himself was arrested, and spent the rest of the war in prison.

On its own, the précis of Mosley's career does little to explain the reverence in which Person X evidently holds him. Mosley didn't come to power; the BUF presented, at best, a second-rate imitation of successful continental fascism. A yawning cultural and social gulf separates Person X, the internet shitposter from a 'low-income family' in regional Australia, and Sir Oswald Mosley, the playboy Sixth Baronet of Ancoats.

Yet, unlike Hitler and Mussolini, Mosley survived the Second World War. After his release from prison, he set about reconstructing an English-speaking fascism for the post-war era, in terms that still resonate today.

Mosley had always been influenced by continental fascism (not least because he'd been funded by both the Italians and the Germans). After the war, he shifted his emphasis from a narrow English nationalism to a broader Europeanism, encapsulated in his phrase 'Europe-a-nation'. Amidst the wreckage left by conflict, he spoke of overcoming economic malaise with a 'third force', fighting both 'Mob' (communism) and 'Money' (the rising American empire).

Though it dismayed some of his older followers, the new orientation positioned Mosley within an intellectual context that would influence the far right for decades. In many countries, fascism had enjoyed mass support — and now its intellectuals were struggling to come to terms with shattering defeat. After 1945, Mosley became part of a milieu of fascist thinkers recasting their doctrine for a new period.

His European focus allowed Mosley to relate to the anxieties arising around post-war immigration from the developing world. Where previously his supporters had addressed 'Britons', now they spoke to 'Europeans' opposed to a supposed influx of non-whites. As Richard C. Thurlow notes, Mosley's Union Movement became, in 1951, the first significant political party to campaign against the 'coloured invasion', filling its newspaper with stories of dope peddling, black crime, and the molestation of white women, and demanding a 'white Brixton'. Later, Mosley cheered on the Notting Hill race riots of 1958, and made overtures to the 'Teddy boy' gangs implicated in anti-immigrant violence.[21]

The significance of Mosley to Person X thus becomes clearer. The BUF's agitation against Jews in Britain bears no direct relevance for an Australian fascist living in New Zealand. But Mosley's later doctrine presented 'Europeanism' as an expansive category, a political ideal as much as a geographical identification. In a similar fashion, Person X could write about defending 'our lands' against 'invaders', even as he stood on the soil that Maori called Aotearoa.

Mosley represents a link between the 'glamour' of the classical era and the strategies of tiny far-right grouplets today — organisations that present comparable ideas, albeit to a much-reduced constituency. Sir Oswald was the handsome playboy who married Diana Mitford in Goebbels' drawing room (at a ceremony attended by Adolf Hitler); he was also the post-war leader of a fringe sect campaigning against immigrants while trying to recruit teenage thugs. He embodies fascist continuity — linking, however tenuously, the age of Hitlerism to the misfits attracted to neo-Nazi groups today.

But whether Person X recognised it or not, Mosley's post-war career also illustrates the distinctive problems facing fascists in the second half of the twentieth century — and indirectly highlights the opportunities presented to them in the very different circumstances prevailing today.

Mosley had pinned his hopes of a political comeback on the expectation of economic downturn, a return of the conditions in which the BUF had grown. In the immediate devastation of the post-war era, Britain did, indeed, experience a revived anti-Semitism, with Mosley addressing a meeting of 3,000 people in 1947 after anti-Jewish riots in Glasgow, Liverpool, and Manchester.

Yet, despite a short recession that year, both Britain and the world economy recovered, entering capitalism's longest-ever period of consistent growth. The resulting political and economic stability was not conducive to the middle-class hysteria upon which fascism depended. Not surprisingly, Mosley's various projects failed to gain traction.

He also struggled against the intense post-war hostility to fascism in general and Nazism in particular. After his release, he was widely seen as a traitor, an apologist for fascist genocide. The public meetings and rallies he sought to hold in the late 1940s were regularly attacked (particularly by Jewish ex-servicemen), so much so that by 1949 Mosley abandoned them and fled overseas.[22]

In that period, and for the rest of his life, he tried and failed to disassociate fascism from the horrors of Nazi Germany. He oscillated between disowning anti-Semitism and embracing it; he rejected any responsibility for the Holocaust, and then grew into, as one historian puts it, 'a central figure in a veritable cottage industry of [Holocaust] revisionism and denial'.[23]

In the 1930s, fascism had not necessarily been beyond the pale in respectable circles, with many establishment politicians expressing an interest in what they saw as the innovative social experiments conducted by Mussolini and Hitler. After 1945, the term became taboo — and only attracted more odium as knowledge of Nazi atrocities circulated more generally.

Increasingly, the Holocaust, the most egregious moral catastrophe of the modern era, functioned as an obstacle hindering not merely those who preached overt fascism, but for anyone advocating the kind of biological racism that reached its denouement in Auschwitz.

For the rest of the twentieth century, fascists in Britain and around the world grappled with the same seemingly intractable problem. The memory of the Six Million rendered overt fascism anathema to most people. The racism they had traditionally used was increasingly unacceptable, in part because of its association with Nazi race science.

But then came the twenty-first century — and new opportunities for the fascist right.

2

'SWEEP IT ALL UP!'

THE WORLD AFTER 9/11

On 11 September 2001, hijacked planes slammed into the Twin Towers and the Pentagon. With the wreckage still smouldering, secretary of defense Donald Rumsfeld mused to a note-taking aide about the strategic opportunities the tragedy offered for America, particularly in relation to his long-held desire for regime change in Iraq.

'Hard to get good case. Need to move swiftly,' he said. 'Near term target needs — go massive — sweep it all up, things related and not.'[1]

The prolonged military conflict that followed reshaped the world. The Brown University Cost of War project estimates that, by November 2018, the US had committed itself to an astonishing \$5.9 trillion on the War on Terror (including direct costs for interventions in Iraq, Syria, Afghanistan, Pakistan, and elsewhere, as well as obligations for future expenditure).[2]

Those conflicts established 'the Muslim' as the West's existential foe in a clash of civilisations. After 9/11, the United States found itself, as Douglas Little put it, 'swamped by a wave of Islamophobia … the media crawled with reports of Muslim plots to destroy America that echoed xenophobic tales from the distant and not-so-distant past …'[3]

'Islamophobia' remains, in some circles, a controversial concept. Critics reject the categorisation of anti-Muslim sentiment as racist, usually on the basis that 'Islam' constitutes a religion rather than a race. Yet 'Judaism' is not a race. Nor is 'Pakistani', nor 'black', nor many of the other descriptors employed by bigots. Biological races do not exist. Or, more exactly, they do not exist other than as categories generated and enforced by racists.

Despite its unfortunate etymology (misleadingly suggestive of a psychological condition), 'Islamophobia' refers to what we might call the racialisation of Islam, its transformation into an essentialist category providing a master explanation for the behaviour of billions of disparate people.

In Person X's writing we find a particularly clear illustration of how, nearly twenty years after 9/11, 'Islam' has become for many an essentialised, almost biological, term.

'It's the birthrates,' he explains, in the opening section of his document. 'If there is one thing I want you to remember from these writings, its [sic] that the birthrates must change.'[4]

He goes on to argue that, 'due to its high fertility rates, [Islam] will grow to replace other peoples and faiths' — a claim that explicitly posits Islam as an inheritable condition, a trait passed from one generation to the other, just like skin colour, or nose size, or any of the other traditional signifiers of racial identity.[5]

That passage exemplifies how Islamophobia has functioned in the post-9/11 world.

In the 1920s and 1930s, a distinctive anti-Semitic tradition circulated throughout most English-speaking countries. Anti-Jewish racism appeared, as a matter of course, in the mainstream press, in the speeches of political candidates, and in cultural productions such as films and novels.

The industrialist Henry Ford, an obsessive anti-Semite, compiled the prevailing stereotypes into his 1920 tract, *The International Jew: the world's foremost problem*, a volume that thus provides a handy illustration. In the book, Ford denounced Jewish immigrants for what he called attempts to 'Judaize the United States' while fantasising that Jewish financiers were shaping the course of history according to an ancient plan. The Jew stood behind the Bolsheviks, but also ran the banking industry: 'poor in his masses,' Ford said, 'he yet controls the world's finances'.[6]

Ford's writings proved, not surprisingly, invaluable to fascists the world over in the 1920s and 1930s. In Germany, *The International Jew* had been through an astonishing six editions by 1922 alone. In 1931, Hitler told a Detroit journalist that he regarded Ford as his hero, and in 1938, Ford was awarded the Grand Cross of the German Eagle, a decoration accompanied by a personal thank-you note from Hitler.[7]

After the Second World War, the Ford company distanced itself from the views of its founder, whose bigotry was no longer politically palatable. The Holocaust, and the experience of Nazism more generally, had fundamentally discredited the anti-Semitic tradition.

Islamophobia, however, didn't have the same associations, even though as far back as 1985, the scholar Edward Said had described it as a prejudice 'nourished at the same stream as anti-Semitism'.[8] Mattias Gardell notes that the medieval Christian hostility to the 'enemies of God' extended from Jews to what were then called 'Moors, Saracens or Red Jews': Muslims, too, were said to worship devils, defame Christian symbols, use children for blasphemous rituals, and so on.[9]

Prior to 9/11, Islamophobia remained a relatively minor current in the West. The War on Terror changed that, normalising a discourse that replicated, almost exactly, the key tropes of pre-war anti-Semitism. Islamophobic bigots linked all Muslims to jihad, precisely as anti-Semites had held all Jews accountable for Bolshevism.

'Maybe most Moslems [sic] peaceful,' tweeted the media magnate Rupert Murdoch, 'but until they recognize and destroy their growing jihadist cancer they must be held responsible.'[10]

After Auschwitz, Ford's reference to a 'Jewish problem' sounded unmistakably sinister. But, after 9/11, Murdoch's employee Bill O'Reilly could repeatedly denounce 'a Muslim problem in the world', a phrase later adopted by Trump.[11]

In the 2000s, only fringe fascists dared use terms like 'Judaisation'. But groups pledging to 'Stop Islamisation' sprung up across Europe and the US, promising (as the American organisation explained their mission) 'to rouse public fears about a vast Islamic conspiracy'.

Once, bigots had railed against the 'the kosher food racket';[12] now Islamophobia fostered new campaigns against halal certification.[13] Old-school racists mocked traditional Jewish clothing; new-style racists campaigned against the burqa.[14]

Almost every aspect of early-twentieth-century anti-Semitism repeated itself in twenty-first-century Islamophobia, often with substantial institutional support. The Centre for American Progress documented a tightly organised and well-funded Islamophobic net-work of pundits, blogs, and organisations operating in the United States, funded by seven charitable founda-tions spending \$42.6 million between 2001 and 2009.[15] Another report by the Council on American-Islamic Relations and the University of California Berkeley's Center for Race and Gender listed 74 Islamophobic groups (including the David Horowitz Freedom Center, the Middle East Forum, the American Freedom Law Center, Jihad Watch, and the Investigative Project on Terrorism) funded to the tune of \$206 million between 2008 and 2013.[16]

Crucially, Islamophobia lacked a direct historical identification with Nazism. It also sounded quite different from the racism fought by civil-rights campaigners and other activists in the 1960s and 1970s. As a result, while the most enthusiastic promoters of Islamophobia came from the right, the new bigotry attracted some figures previously thought of as 'progressive', such as Richard Dawkins, Christopher Hitchens, and Bill Maher.[17]

It's worth exploring one example in detail. In the wake of 9/11, the Italian journalist Oriana Fallaci complained that Muslims 'breed like rats'. In a series of bestselling books, she popularised the 'Eurabia' conspir-acy theory developed by the prolific autodidact Bat Ye'or (Gisele Littman), in which globalists were said to use immigrants to 'Islamise' the continent.

As Matt Carr argues, the Eurabia narrative depends on presenting Muslim immigrants from many different nations as essentially identical, something he calls 'flat-out barking gibberish'. In some iterations, the theory essentially reconstructs an Islamophobic presentation of the *Protocols of the Elders of Zion*, with Islamists presiding over a secret alliance with Third Worldists and neo-communists in 'a powerful jihadist coalition against Western democracies and their allies'.[18]

Yet Fallaci's role in popularising such conspiracies exemplified how Islamophobia enabled the far right to emerge from the shadow of Auschwitz. She had, after all, spent her childhood in a Partisan band fighting Mussolini's troops. She was not recognised as a right-winger — in fact, she enjoyed a reputation as an anti-fascist.

Had such a mad notion as 'Eurabia' centred on a 'Jewish plot', its proponents would, rightfully, have been shunned. Yet versions of the Eurabia idea appeared in work by Melanie Phillips, Bernard Lewis, Niall Ferguson, and many, many other widely published writers.

In his bestselling book *America Alone*, Mark Steyn expanded on the same concept, warning about the 'Muslim world's high birth rate', and telling readers to 'start with demography, because everything does'.[19]

Compare the lines with which Person X begins his manifesto:

It's the birthrates.

It's the birthrates.

It's the birthrates.

Steyn, a Canadian polemicist, belongs to the tradition of racist populism rather than fascism. Nowhere does he argue for his readers to violently destroy their perceived enemies. Nevertheless, the spread of Islamophobia — according to one study, Murdoch's Australian papers published 3,000 negative stories relating to Islam in a single year[20] — equipped genuine fascists like Person X with an important tool: a widely accepted racist conspiracy theory that they could fit to their own ends.

In his manifesto, Person X asks himself a rhetorical question about why, given his belief that all immigrants deserved death, he targeted Muslims in particular.

The decision was, he explains, purely tactical. 'They [Muslims] are the most despised group of invaders in the West,' he says, '[and so] attacking them receives the greatest level of support.'[21]

His focus on demographic change reflects another key development of the post-9/11 era: a new hostility to refugees and migrants. By its nature, the War on Terror intensified the developed world's focus on border policing, generalising Islamophobia into a broader anxiety about race and immigration. David Renton argues that the War on Terror:

served to racialise a wider set of people than just Muslims, making everyone 'white' or 'black', 'Jewish' or 'Hindu'. It … trained mainstream journalists to see minority groups as united around political projects; and [gave] the nod to essentialist views of white ethnicity, in which immigration, above all Muslim immigration, is a collective suicide in the face of a militant enemy.[22]

Again, the experience of the 1930s demonstrates how the process works. In 1938, the leaders of the democratic world had convened a meeting — the so-called Évian Conference — to discuss the refugee crisis produced by Nazi anti-Semitism. Hitler responded by taunting the attendees as hypocrites. If they disapproved of German racism, he mocked, why didn't they welcome refugees to their own countries?

'I can only hope and expect,' he said, 'that the other world, which has such deep sympathy for these criminals [that is, Jews], will at least be generous enough to convert this sympathy into practical aid. We, on our part, are ready to put all these criminals at the disposal of these countries, for all I care, even on luxury ships.'[23]

The resolve of the ostensibly anti-racist democracies to maintain their borders — in other words, their determination to repel desperate people seeking aid

— became, as Hitler understood, a powerful legitimator of Nazi racism.

After the war, Hannah Arendt lamented how the Jews 'whom the persecutor had singled out as scum of the earth ... actually were received as scum of the earth everywhere; those whom persecution had called undesirable became the indésirables of Europe'.[24]

The same phenomenon re-emerged after 9/11, as the rich nations greeted families driven from their homes by military conflict (often, conflict resulting from Western interventions) with detention, harassment, and demonisation. That treatment legitimised further abuse, in precisely the manner Arendt outlined.

Person X called his manifesto 'The Great Replacement', borrowing the title from a 2012 book by the French philosopher Renaud Camus. Camus drew on existing French traditions of anti-immigrant racism (in particular, Jean Raspail's 1973 invasion novel *The Camp of the Saints*), and merged them with the Eurabia thesis to argue that France faced a conspiracy from leftists to destroy the nation via immigration.[25]

Camus' thesis has provided a rallying cry for the right all around the world (even though most of his writing remains untranslated). In Europe, it motivated the German anti-Islam movement Pegida and the fascist group Generation Identity. In 2012, the American alt-right leader Richard Spencer entitled the first edition of his Radix Journal 'The Great Erasure';[26] Canadian alt-right celebrity Lauren Southern produced a YouTube documentary entitled 'The Great Replacement' that received some half a million views.[27] Symptomatically, when American fascists marched at the Unite the Right rally at Charlottesville, they chanted, 'You will not replace us' (or 'Jews will not replace us').

Versions of the argument have appeared in the mainstream, with, for instance, Tucker Carlson (the replacement for Bill O'Reilly on Fox News) warning about 'demographic change' and the 'genocide' facing white men.[28]

But rhetorical support for the theory has mattered less than the reinforcement provided by state policy.

After 9/11, the Bush administration linked immigration enforcement to the fight against terrorism, bringing the various agencies concerned with policing immigration under the umbrella of the newly created and extraordinarily powerful Department of Homeland Security, which received a huge funding boost. That coincided with an expansion in immigrant removals, the rate of which doubled between 2001 and 2011.[29] The process was bipartisan, reaching a crescendo under the Obama administration. The supposedly progressive Barack Obama deported an astonishing 2.7 million people — a figure that amounts to about 1,000 immigrants a day, for eight years.[30]

The growth of what the *Nation* calls the 'deportation machine that Obama built for President Trump' could not help but amplify the rhetoric of the far right. If immigrants weren't dangerous, why was the American state both deporting and imprisoning them? If there was no demographic threat, why was the DHS such a huge agency, boasting more than 48,000 staff devoted exclusively to immigration enforcement?[31]

The practice of government legitimised the rhetoric of the right, just as much as the rhetoric of the right made possible punitive government practices.

After the Second World War, Aimé Césaire published an essay entitled 'Discourse on Colonialism' — in part, an argument about Nazism. In it, Césaire linked fascism to the brutality inflicted on the colonial nations, a brutality that damaged the perpetrators nearly as much as the victims. By supporting repression and torture in Africa or Asia, Europeans legitimated a violent hostility to democracy on their own continent. With each act of imperial cruelty, he concluded, 'civilisation acquires another dead weight, a universal regression takes place, a gangrene sets in, a centre of infection begins to spread'.[32]

Something similar happened during the War on Terror. As the Cost of War Project notes, in Iraq, Afghanistan, and other theatres, American troops detained hundreds of thousands of people, often handing them over for detention to regimes notorious for abuse. Terror suspects were incarcerated without trial, including in Guantanamo Bay where more than one hundred people remain in custody more or less entirely outside the rule of law. Targeted killings, waterboarding, detention without trial: all of these were well established by the early 2000s.

Not surprisingly, political rhetoric within the West became increasingly inflected with what the journalist David Neiwert calls 'eliminationism', a discourse in which dissidents became not opponents to be argued with, but threats to be neutralised or destroyed.

'Everybody got it?' the right-wing cable host Bill O'Reilly asked his listeners in 2005. 'Dissent, fine; undermining, you're a traitor. So all those clowns over at the liberal radio network, we could incarcerate them immediately.'[33]

Now, in one sense, O'Reilly's outburst (and the others like it — Neiwert provides a huge list) was intended as a provocation rather than a genuine proposal. Yet he made such jokes at a time in which real brutality had become state policy.

If enemies could be detained without trial or killed abroad, why not at home? That implicit query provoked the pundit Ann Coulter's response to the detention of John Walker Lindh, an American caught fighting with the Taliban.

'We need to execute people like John Walker,' she said, 'in order to physically intimidate liberals, by making them realise that they can be killed, too.' She later doubled down on the 'gag', suggesting that she actually wanted Lindh burned alive on prime time TV.[34]

The immediate beneficiaries of the new, post-9/11 politics were, by and large, the traditional parties. In the US, the polling company Gallop noted that president Bush's nationwide address after the attacks elicited 'widespread public support for a war against terrorism, as well as the highest presidential job approval rating ever measured by Gallup since it began asking the public for its evaluation of presidents over six decades ago'.[35]

Yet the ability of establishment politicians to capitalise on that consciousness quickly faded, particularly after the Global Financial Crisis. The new racism gave rise to a different kind of right-wing politics, one that Roger Eatwell and Matthew Goodwin describe as 'national populism', that others call 'right-wing populism', and that I've elsewhere dubbed 'outsider anti-elitism'.[36]

Outsider anti-elitism had been on the rise since the 1990s, fuelled by dissatisfaction with the rule of market economics after communism's collapse. But the post 9/11 world allowed it to come into its own, particularly when the Global Financial Crisis (otherwise known as the Great Recession) tore the world economy apart.

Establishment parties were, after all, limited in their deployment of the new discourses about immigration and Muslims by the exigencies of government. They still had to pay lip service, at least, to treaties such as the Refugee Convention; they still needed to work with Muslim leaders to pursue their foreign-policy goals.

Outsider anti-elitists enjoyed far more freedom. Precisely because they presented themselves as insurgents, they could dismiss the norms of the mainstream. Typically, their organisations used racism and conspiracy theories to structure a deep distrust of conventional politicians and institutions: the 'elite', they argued, used Muslim immigration to do down ordinary people. Outsider anti-elitism tapped into fears about a loss of national identity and traditions, spoke to those who felt themselves to be victims of economic reform and free-market economies, and capitalised on the weakening of the bonds between long-established parties and their voting base.

In the United States, for instance, the Tea Party arose out of right-wing opposition to the Obama administration's subsidy package for homeowners facing foreclosure. Though initially backed by major conservative advocacy organisations, it came to express a broader dissatisfaction with politics-as-usual, with one *Washington Post* survey showing that, while 92 per cent opposed Obama, 87 per cent were also dissatisfied with Republican leaders.[37]

Yet this anti-establishment sentiment was very much shaped by Islamophobia and the eliminationist rhetoric promoted by talk radio and, in particular, Fox News. The early Tea Party grew, in part, from the 9/12 Project, a group launched by Fox presenter Glenn Beck. Beck had previously warned of the Federal Emergency Management Agency detaining patriots in camps, denounced the United Nations for seeking to install a One World government, and attacked Obama as a black militant working in cahoots with the Muslim Brotherhood to bring down America.[38]

But despite the racism of most outsider anti-elitists, it would be wrong to label them as fascist. Genuine fascists sought to destroy democracy, so as to create an authoritarian regime based on supposed natural hierarchies. The centrality of violence to their program meant that fascist organisations usually formed a street-fighting force or militia.

By contrast, national populists presented themselves as expanding democracy to the 'plain people'. They did not, for the most part, campaign on the extra-legal suppression of their enemies. They wanted to replace an elite they depicted as morally corrupt and plotting against the populace, but they sought to do so through electoral politics.[39] Despite its conspiratorial and almost insurrectionary rhetoric, the Tea Party, for instance, concentrated in practice on supporting the preselection of socially conservative or populist Republicans. It did not organise fights in the streets.

Nevertheless, the boundary lines between outsider anti-elitism and genuine fascism could become difficult to discern, as the 2016 US presidential election would prove.

3

'HAIL TRUMP!'

FASCIST MEMES

At the end of 2016, the Merriam-Webster dictionary site reported that readers had searched for 'fascism' more than any other word except 'surreal'.[1]

For many, the election of Donald Trump in America signalled an epochal shift — the arrival of the first fascist president. Trump had campaigned, after all, on banning Muslims from entering the US and on building a wall to keep out Mexicans (whom he described as 'rapists' involved in 'drugs' and 'crime').[2] He had used slogans, such as 'America First', associated with historical far-right movements. He had boasted about sexually assaulting women, he had mocked disabled and female reporters, and he had revelled in flouting the conventions of high office.

During the 2016 campaign, and even more so after it, a long list of politicians and commentators described the US president as a 'fascist' (or at least 'fascistic').

'Trump is a fascist,' tweeted Max Boot. 'And that's not a term I use loosely or often. But he's earned it.'[3]

Bret Stephens from *The Wall Street Journal* called Trump's proposal for a 'Muslim registry' 'fascism, plain and simple'; the former Virginia governor Jim Gilmore accused Trump of engaging in 'fascist talk'.[4]

'I'm still not sure it's 100 per cent clear that Donald Trump really understands that he's a neo-fascist,' wrote Michael Tomasky in the *Daily Beast*.[5]

Similar comments came from Madeleine Albright, Matt Yglesias, Timothy Snyder, Jamelle Bouie, Chauncey DeVega, and many others.

Clearly, Trump was not a conventional politician. But a comparison of him with genuine fascists reveals obvious differences. Trump did not, after all, enrol his supporters in a mass movement based on suppressing 'traitors' or the ethnically impure. He presented his racist policies as dependent upon his electoral victory. His crassness and abuse of opponents reflected his background in reality TV rather than any experience of street oration; he showed no interest in staging real-world confrontations with his enemies.

The post-9/11 era saw all political tendencies shift to the right, with social democracy and the mainstream right embracing xenophobia and anti-Muslim racism, even as disaffection with the parties created new populist forces. Trump might be understood as a merger between two previously distinct traditions: the conservatism of the Republican Party right and the outsider anti-elitism of the Tea Party.

Take, for instance, the speech that Trump gave to his supporters in early 2016:

> Hillary Clinton meets in secret with international banks to plot the destruction of US sovereignty in order to enrich these global financial powers, her special-interest friends, and her donors. This election will determine whether we are a free nation or whether we have only the illusion of democracy, but are in fact controlled by a small handful of global special interests rigging the system.[6]

This was not the conventional rhetoric of a Republican. If the comments were not, in and of themselves, racist, they reprised a traditional racist trope — the notion of a sinister clique shaping history in secret — and allowed listeners to draw their own conclusions as to whom exactly (Jews? Muslims? The Illuminati?) the 'special interests' might be.

The speech reflected the influence of outsider anti-elitism on the political mainstream, with the conspiratorial logic underpinning 'Eurabia' or 'The Great Replacement' manifesting not on cable TV but in the stump speech of a presidential candidate.

Again, while Trump did lead his supporters in chants of 'lock her up', his campaign did not embrace the violence so central to fascism. His response to hecklers, often cited as evidence of his fascistic inclinations, actually showed the difference between a populist like Trump and a fascist like Mosley.

'If you see somebody with a tomato, knock the crap out of them,' Trump told supporters in Iowa, in a typical incident.[7] On another occasion, Trump explained that his opponent might be removed from office by those he called 'the Second Amendment people' (that is, gun owners).[8] The rhetoric was deliberately ugly, intended — as with populist eliminationism more generally — to outrage liberals.

But, unlike Mosley, Trump hadn't organised a specially trained group of supporters to attack protesters, nor did he stage the carefully calibrated display of brutality choreographed by the British Union. His statements more resembled the quips of an O'Reilly or a Coulter: a reflection of a coarsened, debased political culture, certainly, but provocations rather than real calls for action.

Trump's victory should more properly be understood as the culmination of a long process by which a racist populism had entered the mainstream and blended into the long-standing right-wing traditions of the Republican Party. Which does not mean that his election was not meaningful for the far right.

'Hail Trump! Hail our people! Hail victory!' said the fascist leader Richard Spencer at a November 2016 meeting of the so-called alt-right, as his listeners responded with Nazi salutes.[9]

The sudden prominence of Spencer, and a score of other more-or-less overt fascists, reflected, among other factors, the new media environment of the twenty-first century, with the internet in general — and social media in particular — providing an ideal medium for the dissemination of fascist ideas.

To understand the advantages of the digital environment to fascists, one need only recall the experience of the far right in the late twentieth century: a period in which would-be recruits often struggled to access fascist texts, let alone connect with others who shared their ideas.

In his memoirs, David Greason (one of the founders of a tiny Australian fascist groupuscle in the 1970s) discusses his struggles to locate a copy of *The Protocols of Zion*. Eventually, he found one in the offices of the League of Rights, a longstanding organisation of anti-Semitic conspiracy theorists:

> Three poky rooms, two walls of books, a tatty curtain, an old man and an old woman. There may have been a picture of the Queen somewhere; I can't remember … The bookshop doubled as a storeroom for dust. Volumes that hadn't been disturbed for centuries

were stacked up to the ceiling. Wonky old parcels of booklets, some with their wonky old contents spilling out, were perched on shelves like booby traps.[10]

By contrast, in his manifesto, Person X gives readers a simple answer to the question of where he researched and developed his beliefs: 'The internet, of course.'[11]

As early as 1996, a would-be fascist could log onto Stormfront, the site described by the Anti-Defamation League as 'a veritable supermarket of online hate, stocking its shelves with many forms of anti-Semitism and racism'. By 2005, Stormfront ranked in the top 1 per cent of sites on the World Wide Web;[12] by 2008, it was attracting 40,000 unique users a day.[13]

Support for fascism was often dispersed geographically, with the far right typically strongest in small towns, rural areas, or the outskirts of cities. In the past, even if a fascist group maintained an office in such places, potential recruits felt, understandably, embarrassed to be seen inside it.

The forums on Stormfront and similar sites could, however, be accessed anonymously by anyone from anywhere. The internet encouraged visitors to discuss posts, so that casual browsers quickly found themselves debating other readers in the comment threads.

It might even be said that the structure of the internet — interactive yet undemocratic — replicated the characteristic fascist organisational form. A site like Stormfront remained entirely under the control of its moderator who, like the traditional fascist leader, relied on dictates to keep an atomised membership together. Yet individuals could feel, through their involvement in the forums, a sense of belonging, a feeling of participation in something bigger than themselves. By facilitating debates (in comments threads or elsewhere), a fascist page could foster the development of cadres, as participants became more confident in their arguments.

Online interactivity provided a substitute for the real-life meetings that fascists often found difficult to stage. The Islamophobia and xenophobia circulating in the mainstream could be concentrated and intensified in the strange semi-privacy of a web forum, since individuals who might hesitate about joining a racist street march could denounce Muslim refugees in a digital discussion with much less fear of condemnation. As the Australian academic Andrew Jakubowicz noted, the online environment enhanced the 'psychological dimensions of anonymity, disengagement and dis-inhibition', which gave activists far more latitude to suggest physical violence against ethnic minorities and 'traitors'.[14]

In other words, the internet allowed activists of the far right to dissolve the distinction between right-wing populism and genuine fascism. The emergence of social media intensified the process, simply by making an equivalent functionality an everyday part of ordinary people's lives. With the normalisation of Facebook, Twitter, and Reddit, fascists no longer needed supporters to seek out exotic destinations like Stormfront: the far right could present its content on platforms that their recruits were already using.

Furthermore, fascists began to incorporate the distinctive sensibility of troll culture.

Most commentators associate trolling with 4chan, a forum launched in 2003 ostensibly for enthusiasts of anime, comics, games, and similar pursuits. The 4chan users developed meming and many other now-ubiquitous facets of internet culture, but they also created a cruel humour directed at those judged to have transgressed the unwritten codes of online behaviour.[15]

4chan was not, at first, particularly political. Its anonymous members (known as 'anons') sought 'lulz' — the knowing laughter produced by adolescent pranks. But, perhaps inevitably, those lulz often came at the expense of conventional targets such as women, people of colour, and gays.

Trolling had always involved transgression, with anons priding themselves on their indifference to the sentiments of normies. To take a particularly grotesque example, an early campaign centred on systematic harassment of a suicide victim's parents.[16] Because of the emphasis on flouting social and political taboos, the 4chan boards filled with porn (including child porn), racial slurs, violent imagery, and the like. An indifference to conventional ethics or etiquette bonded anons, as Richard Seymour noted, over a kind of collective, escalating glee, on the basis that 'none of us is as cruel as all of us'.[17]

The opportunities that troll culture presented for ideological fascists might best be illustrated by the success of *The Daily Stormer*, a Nazi site that took the Stormfront idea into the twenty-first century. Its editor, a man called Andrew Anglin, set out, as one journalist explained, to 'make hate fun' by adopting 4chan's sensibilities.[18]

A *Daily Stormer* style guide leaked to *The Huffington Post* outlined the project. 'The tone of the site should be light,' Anglin told his potential contributors:

> The unindoctrinated should not be able to tell if we are joking or not. There should also be a conscious awareness of mocking stereotypes of hateful racists. I usually think of this as self-deprecating humor — I am a racist making fun of stereotype [sic] of racists, because I don't take myself super-seriously. This is obviously a ploy and I actually do want to gas kikes. But that's neither here nor there.[19]

Where, for instance, Stormfront presented itself with po-faced solemnity, *The Daily Stormer* used, for a while, a header in which Pokemon characters gambolled alongside Hitler. According to O'Brien, Anglin distributed Nazi memes through 4chan (and its replacement, 8chan) — and then watched as they dispersed 'to a more "mainstream" conservative readership, often through transfer points such as *Breitbart*'.[20] The disinhibition fostered by sites like 8chan eroded revulsion at the Holocaust or fascism more generally, with gags celebrating the Nazis circulating as simply another source of ironic lulz.

But, of course, they weren't. As one 8chan user explained, 'At some point, shit went from, "I'm just pretending to be a racist psycho," to "I actually am a white nationalist lunatic."'[21]

At its peak, *The Daily Stormer* reached something like 2 million readers a month. Yet online influence was not the same as real-world popularity. For fascism to re-emerge as a mainstream political current, its ideologues needed to bring their supporters out from their computers and onto the streets.

In the immediate aftermath of Trump's election, the far right's swollen online presence made that seem a genuine possibility. Trump had appointed *Breitbart*'s Steve Bannon (an admirer of the Italian 'esoteric' fascist Julius Evola)[22] as the White House chief strategist, and Sebastian Gorka (a supporter of the fascist Hungarian Guard)[23] as his deputy assistant. His victory had brought considerable attention to the alt-right, with many of its leaders suddenly thrust into the international spotlight to hold forth on their racial theories.

The most important attempt to transform internet traffic into street activism came via the Unite the Right rally at Charlottesville in August 2017. The protest, ostensibly against the removal of a statue honouring the confederate leader Robert E Lee, received the imprimatur of fascist organisations throughout America, including the Traditionalist Worker Party, Identity Evropa, and long-standing hate groups like the KKK and the National Socialist Movement. But most of the energy for the event came from the new celebrities of the alt-right. The key organiser was a white supremacist, Jason Kessler; the advertised speakers included Richard Spencer, Matthew Heimbach from the fascist Traditionalist Worker Party, the Holocaust denier 'Augustus Invictus', the racist podcaster Mike Enoch (producer of *The Daily Shoah*), the anti-Semitic online activist Tim Gionet (known as 'Baked Alaska'), the neo-Nazi Christopher Cantwell, and others.[24]

Andrew Anglin from *The Daily Stormer* described what was at stake: 'Although the rally was initially planned in support of the Lee Monument … it has become something much bigger than that. It is now an historic rally, which will serve as a rallying point and battle cry for the rising Alt-Right movement.'

At first, the Unite the Right organisers believed they'd staged a triumph, as they gathered to chant fascist slogans like 'Blood and Soil' and 'Jews Will Not Replace Us!'. On its live blog of the event, *The Daily Stormer* crowed, 'We have an army! This is the beginning of a war!'[25]

Donald Trump's lackadaisical response blaming 'many sides' for the death of the anti-racist Heather Heyer emboldened the fascists further, with Anglin's publication declaring that 'Trump comments were good'.

Yet, rather than translating online popularity into ongoing real-world activism, Unite the Right exposed the contradictions that the internet had papered over.

In the desperate 1930s — in societies gripped by political and economic turmoil — fascist violence had appealed to the middle class both as a means and an end. Street battles provided meaning and solidarity in a time of chaos, while the 'revolutionary' aims of fascism promised salvation to despairing people.

But America in 2017 was not Weimar Germany, no matter how the effects of the Global Financial Crisis lingered. Unite the Right did not appeal to the Tea Party crowd or Fox News viewers, or other populists mobilised behind Trump. Such folk might have believed that Muslims were introducing sharia by stealth, and that rapists and gangbangers were entering the country across the Mexican border. But they were not desperate enough to enlist in *The Daily Stormer*'s war, and did not feel impelled to join the few hundred (mostly younger) activists who rallied in Charlottesville behind the fascist banners.

Nor was there a section of the ruling elite prepared to back street fighters in the way that Lord Rothermere had briefly supported Mosley. The militant union movement that Rothermere had feared did not exist in 2017, with industrial disputation so much in decline as to render a paramilitary anti-labour force entirely superfluous, even for the most paranoid industrialist.

As the anti-fascist protests grew, Trump moved to distance himself from the alt-right and from Steve Bannon, who had reportedly scripted his initial ambivalent response to Unite the Right. Within a week, he had fired Bannon, whom he thereafter denounced as 'Sloppy Steve'.[26]

In online forums and social media, fascists could mask their true nature, disguising themselves as shit-posters and trolls. But the murder of Heather Heyer by a white supremacist forced attendees at Unite the Right to confront fascist violence in a way that sharing memes behind their computers did not.

By taking to the streets, the far right made themselves a target. In the weeks after Charlottesville, anti-fascists redoubled their efforts, and it became apparent that the alt-right would not again be able to assemble in public without arousing massive opposition.

Many of the Unite the Right attendees were publicly identified by photos or video footage, and were thus forced either to embrace their fascism in public or (more often) to hastily disavow it. Either way, they lost their reputations, their friends, and their jobs.

Very quickly, the full scale of the catastrophe the fascists had wrought for themselves became clear. Identity Evropa shed its central cadres in pursuit of respectability.[27] The head of the National Socialist Movement handed over leadership to a black civil-rights activist in a bid to duck lawsuits.[28] The Traditionalist Worker Party collapsed, after a bizarre internal schism connected to an affair between Heimbach (who was briefly jailed) and the partner of his deputy, Matt Parrott.[29]

Jason Kessler became, according to the Southern Poverty Law Center, a 'social pariah' in Charlottesville. Richard Spencer cancelled much of his subsequent speaking tour because of protests, and was banned from using Paypal to receive donations. 'Antifa is winning,' he lamented.[30]

'Augustus Invictus' fell out with various organisations with which he'd been associated, including the hate group American Guard, which expelled him for his 'poisonous ideas'. Mike Enoch began feuding with other fascists when leaked personal information revealed his wife to be Jewish. (He later separated from her.) 'Baked Alaska', like many other far-right celebrities, lost his social media accounts — and responded with a much-mocked online meltdown. Christopher Cantwell earned the title 'the Crying Nazi' after he broke down sobbing on video at the prospect of being arrested. *The Daily Stormer* struggled to locate a hosting service, eventually retreating to the dark web, and its editor, Andrew Anglin, fled (purportedly to Cambodia).[31]

Subsequent attempts by fascists to take to the streets drew pitiful numbers. Perhaps 200 attended a march in Shelbyville, Tennessee, while other advertised events simply didn't take place.[32] The Unite the Right 2 rally, an anniversary event organised by Kessler, attracted maybe 20 people. A later Boston rally mobilised a mere handful.[33]

American fascism hadn't disappeared. But its key figures learned, to their great frustration, that they couldn't convert their online support into a conventional political movement as easily as they had hoped.

Such was the context in which Person X developed his own strategy for bridging the gulf between fascism's online strength and its real-world weakness. That strategy was terrorist murder.

4

'SCREW YOUR OPTICS!'

THE CHRISTCHURCH STRATEGY

'Screw your optics, I'm going in.' This was the message posted on Gab by a man called Robert Bowers, just before he killed seven people in the Tree of Life Synagogue in Pittsburgh.[1]

The phrase became a meme on the far right, one that Person X incorporated into his own final 8chan post.

'Optics' refers to a debate that divided American fascists after Charlottesville. As Unite the Right unravelled, Anglin attacked those alt-right activists who wanted more such marches (in particular, those connected with the Traditionalist Worker Party) as LARPers (live-action role-players). They were embarrassing misfits who discredited the movement.

'We need to remain in the realm of the hip, cool, sexy, fun,' he said. 'We need to speak to the culture.'[2]

Fascists, he insisted, needed to continue propagandising online, developing cadres who might eventually influence real politics.

'We are in no way ready to "take to the streets". We have absolutely zero infrastructure. We do not have a huge pool of reliable, competent people. We do not have any stable organizations … We do not really have much of anything at all.'[3]

His opponents in the TWP and elsewhere responded by labelling him, in the charming parlance of the alt-right, an 'optics cuck' (a reference to the 'cuckold porn' genre in which white men watched black men have sex with their wives). They claimed that the alt-right had to continue moving into the streets. Wearing uniforms and battling leftists conveyed an attractive image of strength, they said.

'Our conviction,' explained the TWP's Matt Parrott, 'is that a political movement which fails to occupy public space, which lacks the strength to stand its ground in public, is stillborn. That fight isn't optional, and it's not one we could or should forfeit on account of "optics".'[4]

The LARPers lost the so-called 'Optics War'. By Unite the Right 2, fascists could no longer occupy public space, since counter-protests blocked their every attempt. Political frustration over that failure formed the backdrop to the feud in which the TSP disintegrated after Heimbach, quite literally, cuckolded Parrott.

But if Anglin won, his victory was largely pyr-rhic. The increased attention on the fascist scene after Charlottesville made even the old online activism more difficult, as the big social media companies responded to pressure to police their services. Key fascist leaders lost much of their digital presence — in many cases, retreating to niche platforms like Gab.

In a context of widespread demoralisation, Person X offered a third alternative in the Optics War. As the 'screw your optics' slogan suggested, Person X scorned Anglin's commitment to exclusively online fascism. Yet he also rejected Unite the Right-style rallies and other attempts to build a conventional political movement.

He embraced, instead, terrorism. He was not, of course, the first to do so. In his manifesto, Person X claimed he took 'inspiration from Knight Justiciar [Anders] Breivik', the man who killed 77 people in Norway in 2011.[5] He even claimed (probably falsely) to have received endorsement for his own attack from Breivik's (probably fictitious) organisation.

But Person X developed a distinctive understanding of the strategic value of terror. His murders were, he said, vengeance against those whom he called 'invaders', and a contribution to their extermination. More importantly, they would 'show the effect of direct action, lighting a path forward for those that wish to follow'.[6]

The claim that terrorism might 'light a path' goes

back to the nineteenth century, when anarchists like Johann Most advocated so-called propaganda by the deed, in which daring blows against oppressors supposedly inspired the masses into imitative revolt.[7]

The strategy rarely worked in the way that Most claimed, simply because of the gulf between its democratic rhetoric and its elitist practice. Even on occasions when the people approved of an attack on a tyrant or industrialist, they weren't necessarily stirred into action. They were as likely to conclude that politics could be left to those revolutionary 'heroes' who would take action on their behalf.

Person X's version of the methodology made, at first glance, much less sense than Most's.

The original exponents of propaganda by deed planned their actions to generate maximum sympathy, targeting, for instance, particularly cruel autocrats or capitalists widely despised by the populace.

That was not what Person X did. He did not bomb a symbolic target, or kidnap an unpopular politician, or stage a dramatic skyjacking, or something of that sort. He slaughtered peaceful worshippers — an atrocity calculated to repel even many who might otherwise have sympathised with Person X's racism.

The horror and disgust expressed by New Zealanders was entirely predictable. If ordinary people did not support fascists marching in the street, they were scarcely likely to applaud cold-blooded murder.

Not surprisingly, commentators judged Person X a fantasist, deluded by his own propaganda into believing that mass slaughter would somehow inspire a fascist revolution. But they did not grasp how Person X's strategy reflected a broader debate.

Despite his rhetoric about the masses, Person X did not intend his manifesto for the public. He deliberately sought to baffle 'normies' via his shitposting, with the document studded with 8chan humour.[8] Rather than addressing ordinary people, Person X wrote his document for the fascist right, going out of his way to exclude those who couldn't grasp the internet irony in which the fascist right was steeped.

In that sense, he belonged on Anglin's side in the 'Optics War'. He recognised the importance of internet culture to the far right: 'memes,' he said, 'have done more for the ethnonationalist movement than any manifesto'.[9] Yet he also argued, explicitly, that memes were not enough — and he included in his manifesto the fascist kitsch that Anglin despised.

The document contains, for instance, no fewer than three sentimental poems: works by Dylan Thomas, Rudyard Kipling, and William Ernest Henley, presented entirely without irony. It concludes with photos of blonde women staring at babies, images of domestic harmony quite at odds with the pornographic sensibilities of 4chan, 8chan or *The Daily Stormer*. Person X even breaks into faux-Romantic prose, advising his readers to consider death 'as certain as the setting of the sun at evenfall'.[10]

Thus, while much of the manifesto reads like a shit-post, other sections drip with the maudlin sincerity that shitposters despise. It blends the opposing positions in the 'Optics War' into a third, and different, perspective.

The synthesis was possible because of the form of terror that Person X embraced — one with a distinctive place in contemporary Western culture.

In 1966, a man called Charles Whitman murdered his mother and his wife, and then, carrying an arsenal of weapons, climbed atop a 307-foot tower at the University of Texas in Austin to open fire on students and staff. In total, he killed 17 people.

Today, we might be horrified at Whitman's rampage, but it does not baffle us. We are accustomed to gunmen shooting up schools or workplaces. Yet, prior to 1966, such crimes were almost unknown.

Discussing what he calls 'autogenic massacres', the forensic psychiatrist Paul Mullen claims that they 'do not even begin to appear until the twentieth century and only emerge as a recurring theme in the last thirty years'.[11]

The statistics are contested, since much depends on how one defines a 'massacre', a 'rampage', or a 'mass killing'. But, in the fifty years prior to the University of Texas murders, records show only 25 public mass shootings in which four or more people died in the United States.[12]

By contrast, a list compiled by *Mother Jones* identifies at least 110 such incidents since 1982. 'They are occurring more often,' the magazine concludes. 'An analysis of this database by researchers at Harvard University, further corroborated by a different study from the FBI, determined that mass shootings have tripled in frequency in recent years.'[13]

Furthermore, autogenic massacres have developed well-defined, almost rigid, generic conventions. The killer makes detailed preparations, stockpiling guns and ammunition, and often assembling a uniform or costume. He writes a note or shoots a video, detailing his grievances and complaints. He finds a concentration of people and opens fire, shooting indiscriminately until he turns his weapon on himself, is slain by police, or (more rarely) captured.

This, says Mullen, is 'a relatively new form of behaviour in western cultures but one that has now acquired a clear social script and which appears to be becoming increasingly frequent'.

Mullen and others have put considerable effort into assembling psychological profiles of shooters. After analysing a number of surviving killers, Mullen concludes, perhaps not unexpectedly, that 'they had personality problems and were, to put it mildly, deeply troubled people'. But then he adds, 'Most perpetrators of auto-genic massacres do not, however, appear to have active psychotic symptoms at the time, and very few even have histories of prior contact with mental health services.'

In any case, individual profiling cannot explain the emergence of the gun-massacre script — why 'deeply troubled' people carry out massacres when they didn't fifty years earlier — nor its development. In 1986, for instance, mass shootings broke out in a string of work-places across the US; in 1997, the phenomenon spread to schools.[14]

In his book *Going Postal*, Mark Ames offers a social and historical analysis, associating what he calls 'rage murder' with profound changes in American society. 'The rage murder is new,' he argues. 'It appeared under Reagan, during his cultural and economic revolution, and it expanded in his aftermath.'[15]

He focuses, in particular, on the workplace shootings of the 1980s, which began with a number of massacres carried out by postal employees (hence his title). At the time, the service was under particular pressure from what we'd now call neoliberal reform, as redundancies, cost-cutting, and productivity increases fostered stress and insecurity among the workforce. When Ames inter-viewed massacre survivors, they sometimes expressed a surprising sympathy for the shooters. The experience of work — the activity that most people spend most of their lives performing — had become a nightmare, as job satisfaction gave way to perpetual anxiety, and the solidarity between employees collapsed into bullying and minor harassment.

Ames says that workplace massacres migrated into the US school system in the 1990s, precisely because the education system manifested the worst aspects of the Reaganite workplace culture. There was, he argues, the 'continuity of misery and entrapment from school to office':

> Even physically, they look alike and act on the mind in a similar way: the overhead fluorescent lights, the economies-of-scale-purchased industrial carpeting and linoleum floors, the stench of cleaning chemicals in the restrooms, the same stalls with the same latches and the same metal toilet paper holders.[16]

Contextualising the crimes in this way doesn't mean understanding them as exclusively (or even primarily) goal-driven. Autogenic massacres do not involve the oppressed striking back against their oppressors. On the contrary, one reason they resist analysis is that they often seem so undirected, with the killer opening fire on a crowd, or targeting complete strangers.

An autogenic massacre becomes more explicable if we focus on the act itself rather than its outcome — if, that is, we confront the possibility that, for the perpetrator, the point of the killing lies in the killing itself.

In his classic essay 'Why Men Love War', William Broyles, Jr discusses how much he — and other Vietnam veterans he knew — had enjoyed armed combat:

> As anyone who has fired a bazooka or an M-60 machine gun knows, there is something to that power in your finger, the soft, seductive touch of the trigger. It's like the magic sword, a grunt's Excalibur: all you do is move that finger so imperceptibly just a wish flashing across your mind like a shadow, not even a full brain synapse, and poof! in a blast of sound and energy and light a truck or a house or even people disappear, everything flying and settling back into dust.[17]

The passage describes violence as an end, not a means, with the almost magical experience of power unrelated to any outcomes. Broyles and his friends enjoyed killing — irrespective of whether that killing helped win the war.

He continues:

> Part of the love of war stems from its being an experience of great intensity ... War replaces the difficult gray areas of daily life with an eerie, serene clarity. In war you usually know who is your enemy

and who is your friend, and are given means of dealing with both … War is an escape from the everyday into a special world where the bonds that hold us to our duties in daily life — the bonds of family, community, work, disappear. In war, all bets are off.'[18]

Another veteran describing combat in Vietnam to the psychiatrist Jonathan Shay spoke of something very similar. 'I felt like a god, this power flowing through me,' he said.[19]

By walking into school with an assault rifle, or opening fire in a crowded street, the damaged men that Mullen describes could experience, for an instant, a power and intensity entirely absent from their everyday lives. In a sense, it doesn't matter who they shoot — they feel godlike because they are shooting someone.

That perhaps illuminates the gendering of rampage killings, crimes overwhelmingly committed by men. The rage murderer takes up his gun not simply because he feels disempowered, but also because of his particular understanding of that disempowerment, his sense of it almost as a slight.

Hannah Arendt notes that rage doesn't arise in response to an incurable disease, or to an earthquake, or 'to social conditions which seem to be unchangeable'. Instead, she says, it erupts only when someone believes 'that conditions could be changed and are not'.[20]

Men and boys learn to associate masculinity with autonomy, control, and dominance. Their inability to assert such things — and the ensuing sense of their inadequacy alongside other, more successful men — might feel like an existential wrong, sufficient to make them crave the distinctly masculine power they identify with violence. The socialisation of women and girls, by contrast, presents disempowerment as naturally feminine — making, perhaps, a gun rampage a less obvious response (than, say, forms of self-harm).

Both Italian fascism and German National Socialism recruited heavily from returned soldiers. Fascist groups appealed to veterans by attributing wartime suffering to internal enemies and by promising to root them out. But they also fetishised the experience of war itself, presenting it as constitutive of a new fascist identity.

In 1914, in an earlier era of economic dislocation, a surprising proportion of the population had welcomed hostilities partly as an antidote to a peacetime they had experienced as stultifying and inhuman. As the historian Eric Leed explains, 'It was commonly felt that with the declaration of war, the populations of European nations had left behind an industrial civilisation with its problems and conflicts, and were entering a sphere of action ruled by authority, discipline, comradeship, and common purpose.'[21]

Peace meant atomisation, alienation, and isolation, with men and women impersonal cogs in the gears of industry. War offered meaning, excitement, and adventure. Modern society was emasculating, dominated by those that the poet Rupert Brooke called 'half-men', while combat restored a traditional virility.

As Julian Grenfell, another soldier poet (and Great War casualty), put it in his poem 'Into Battle', 'And he is dead who will not fight/And who dies fighting has increase.' — lines that, typically, present war as an antidote to the bloodless tedium of everyday life.

The conclusion of his poem reads like a hymn to the berserker state of the rage murderer:

And when the burning moment breaks,
And all things else are out of mind,
And only joy of battle takes
Him by the throat, and makes him blind ...

In Germany, nationalist intellectuals took the ecstasy that some men found in combat and gave it a particular political content, offering war almost as a foretaste of the new *völkisch* regime.

'This war is not the end but the prelude to violence,' declared the veteran and writer Ernst Jünger. 'It is the forge in which the new world will be hammered into new borders and communities. New forms want to be filled with blood, and power will be wielded with a hard fist. The war is a great school, and the new man will bear our stamp … The festival is about to begin, and we are its princes.'[22]

In a very different context, Person X adopted a recognisably similar project.

Mullen used the term 'autogenic' to describe massacres driven by psychopathology or personal (rather than political) problems. The killings carried out by Person X were not autogenic — they were, as he says in his document, a politically motivated terrorist attack.

But he used them to rewrite the massacre script, injecting political content into an apolitical form.

In an important essay about 4chan, Dale Beran emphasises the centrality of competition and humiliation to the culture that grew from the site. He points out how many of the terms popularised by troll culture emphasised status ('fail' and 'win', 'alpha' males and 'beta cucks'), arguing that the channers developed an entire sensibility to cloak a sense of gendered inadequacy, an inability to function beyond the computer screen.[23] The description captures precisely the kind of people likely to be fascinated with the 'burning moment' of a rage massacre — that instant when the emasculated loser experiences godlike masculine power. That propensity was accentuated if the loser in question had been exposed to the ideas of fascism, with their emphasis on violence as redemption.

By exploiting his core constituency's yearning for the dominance and control they associated with gun violence,

Person X sought to transform future autogenic massacres into acts of fascist terror. That was why he so consciously situated himself within a lineage of mass murders.

As we have seen, Person X referred to Robert Bowers, the Tree of Life murderer. He enthused about the man he called 'Knight Justiciar Breivik'. He also named other fascist or racist killers: Luca Traini, who opened fire on African migrants in Italy; Dylann Roof, who killed eight people in Charleston; Anton Lundin Pettersson, who murdered three in a school in Sweden; and Darren Osborne, who rammed his car into pedestrians near the Finsbury Park Mosque in London.

The establishment of a tradition mattered, since tradition shaped the specific form of the rage-murder script.

In May 2014, a 24-year-old man named Elliot Rodger went on a massacre in Isla Vista, California, eventually killing six people. In some respects, Rodger resembled the stereotype of the youthful rampage killer, an unhappy individual obsessed by his lack of social and sexual status, and consumed by fantasies of violent revenge.

Yet Rodger belonged to an online community of 'incels', men who gathered on Reddit and elsewhere to discuss the elaborate, and deeply misogynistic, belief system by which they explained their 'involuntary celibacy'. Rodger and his peers believed themselves unfairly deprived of sex by attractive women they called 'Stacys', who threw themselves at alpha males or 'Chads'. Their ideas drew tacitly on far-right ideologies (in particular, in their sense of feminism as a form of social engineering) without necessarily making that commitment explicit.[24]

Before Rodger took himself and his gun to the Alpha Phi sorority, he uploaded a video explaining the nature of what he dubbed the 'Day of Retribution'. Describing himself as 'the supreme gentleman', he claimed he had 'no choice but to exact revenge on the society' that had 'denied' him sex.[25]

'If we can't solve our problems,' he said, 'we must DESTROY our problems ... One day incels will realise their true strength and numbers, and will overthrow this oppressive feminist system.'[26]

In the aftermath of the murders, Rodger became an object of fascination in incel forums. Members applauded his rampage, reposting his videos or image, and quoting from his manifesto. Because incel culture shared the sensibility (and even some of the members) of 4chan and 8chan, much of that enthusiasm undoubtedly came from shitposters. But internet irony ultimately made no difference, for, in April 2018, a man called Alek Minassian posted a statement on Facebook.

'The Incel Rebellion has already begun! We will overthrow all the Chads and Stacys! All hail the Supreme Gentleman Elliot Rodger!'[27] He then drove a van into female pedestrians on the streets of Toronto, killing ten and wounding many more.

Christopher Sean Harper-Mercer, responsible for nine murders in a community college in Oregon in 2015, left a note in which he praised Rodger,[28] as did Nikolas Cruz, who killed 17 people at Marjory Stoneman Douglas High School.[29]

Rodger had given a particular set of troubled young men a pseudo-political rationale for their violence. Person X sought to do the same, but on a more explicitly fascist basis.

To that end, he thought carefully about how best to inject political content into the rituals associated with massacres. He performed the generic elements of the traditional script in a deliberate and careful manner: writing a farewell, taking pictures of his arsenal, posting a document, and so on. But he gave each of them a distinctly fascist twist.

Rather than a list of personal grievances, he created a political manifesto. Instead of simply posting photos of his guns, he uploaded images of weapons painted with slogans. Where other mass shooters recorded the moment before an attack, Person X live-streamed his killings, thus creating a ghastly record designed to circulate online.

Yet, even as he prepared to perform the most real act imaginable — the taking of human life — he retained the ironic sensibility of the internet right. His video began with him shouting, 'Remember lads, subscribe to

PewDiePie', thus embedding a right-wing meme among the footage of real deaths. The text on his guns invoked obscure people and events significant to fascists. (He mentioned, for instance, the Battle of Tours in 732.) But they also featured the phrase 'Kebab Remover', the title of a Serbian song taken up as a meme by the alt-right.

'Even the massacre itself,' noted *Salvage* magazine, 'from the scrawls on the weapons to the track played by the murderer before his assault began, was conducted in such a way as to induce ripples of exultation among the anons.'[30]

The critique made by Anglin of fascist LARPers centred on the public perception of their street marches. On Gab, Anglin had explained how 'watching a bunch of "Alt-Right" fat guys in costumes get shouted down in the street and laughed at … hurts the morale of our own guys … [and] takes away from things that we've been doing successfully in the propaganda sphere'.[31]

While rejecting the online-only strategy, Person X also recognised the inability of small fascist groups to translate their online support into traditional political activism. By conducting a horrendous massacre, he found a way to present earnest fascist propaganda in ways that no one would dare laugh at.

In his reshaping of rage murder — injecting a conscious political element into the already-existing massacre script — Person X hoped to set in motion a cascading sequence of atrocities, in which young men (on the fringes of the fascist movement or at least already vaguely sympathetic to far-right ideas), would individually decide to, as he put it, 'stop shitposting and make a real-life effort', with each murder inspiring murders to come. After all, according to the *New York Times*, 'at least a third of white extremist killers since 2011 were inspired by others who perpetrated similar attacks, professed a reverence for them or showed an interest in their tactics'.[32]

That was the sense in which Person X was lighting a path forward: not so much inspiring people by his ideas (though he clearly hoped to do that), but fascinating them with 'the enticing urge to destroy'.

He was, as *Salvage* argued, using 'the language of memes to identify himself and his belonging, and to excite and win support from a growing, paradoxical entity: an online community of the lone-wolfish'.[33]

It has already worked. In April 2019, a message appeared on 8chan using Person X's name and linking to a manifesto. 'What I've learned here is priceless,' the anon wrote, and then added, 'a livestream will begin shortly.'[34] Soon, a gunman began shooting at worshippers at a synagogue in Poway, California. After he was captured, one person lay dead and several others were injured.

In his manifesto, the alleged perpetrator explained that, '[Person X] was a catalyst for me personally. He showed me that it could be done. And that it needed to be done.' By attacking a synagogue, the Poway shooter showed, once again, the connection between Islamophobia and anti-Semitism.

Person X had denied an animus against Jews, in a passage that led some commentators to wonder if he in fact rejected the National Socialist preoccupation with the so-called 'Jewish Question'. Yet Person X's disavowal was not what it seemed.

'A Jew living in Israel is no enemy of mine,' he wrote, 'so long as they do not seek to subvert or harm my people.'[35]

The formulation was not, in fact, incompatible with fascist anti-Semitism, since Hitler had briefly contemplated the relocation of Jews in German or conquered territory into an ethno-state.[36] In any case, while Person X approved of Jews living in Israel, his attitude to Jews in 'non-Jewish' countries could be inferred from his attitude to Muslims, whom he regarded as interlopers to be killed.

The Poway shooter found no difficulty in making that connection. In his manifesto, the Poway killer discussed how he'd first tried to set fire to a mosque before attacking a synagogue. Both actions were, he said, attempts to cleanse the nation of 'invaders'.

As well as copying Person X's argument, the Poway killer's document mimicked his style, sprinkling memes among its arguments. Like Person X, the perpetrator live-streamed his attack (though the recording failed).

Like Person X, he spoke of inspiring others to commit further murders.

'Every anon reading this needs to carry out attacks,' he said.[37]

As Charlie Warzel noted in *The New York Times*, fascist shootings had become 'sickeningly standardised' to a template tailored for the internet.[38]

Disturbingly, the incident showed that the audience also understood the script. The first response to the Poway killer's post came from another user who urged him to get 'a high score' — by killing lots of people.[39]

A few months later, in August 2019, a man opened fire in a Walmart in El Paso. He, too, wrote a document — this time, denouncing Hispanics rather than Muslims or Jews, and posted it on 8chan. It began, 'In general, I support the Christchurch shooter and his manifesto.'

Again, the anons cheered. 'Things ARE accelerating,' wrote one, 'and attacks are happening with increasing frequency.'

The strategy of Person X seemed to be working.

5

'FORESTS, LAKES, MOUNTAINS, AND MEADOWS'

ECOFASCISM AND ACCELERATIONISM

Nothing in Person X's document has spurred as much confusion as his references to the environment and environmentalism. 'I ... consider myself an Eco-fascist by nature,' he wrote.[1]

Many conservatives used his self-description as an eco-fascist to cordon off Person X from the ideas of the right. He couldn't be a right-winger, they said, because he'd identified himself as an environmentalist — and environmentalists belonged on the left.[2]

Others suggested that his comments about climate change revealed mental confusion, evidence that his manifesto should be taken less as a coherent ideological statement and more as a grab bag of pathologies. But in the context of the ongoing strategic debate among fascists, Person X's professed 'environmentalism' made perfect sense, particularly given the affinity between the far right and a certain ecological tradition.

In many countries, environmentalism developed alongside the anti-immigration movement, with the same personnel sometimes involved in both. In the United States, for example, the lawyer Madison Grant founded the National Parks Association, the Save the Redwoods League, and the New York Zoological Society, helped establish the Denali National Park in Alaska and Everglades National Park in Florida — and wrote *The Passing of the Great Race*, a book that Hitler described as his bible. Grant's interest in conservation and his interest in eugenics stemmed from a similar source: a belief that races were akin to natural species, and thus needed to be tended and preserved.[3]

In her bestselling book *H is for Hawk*, Helen MacDonald writes of seeing deer congregating on inhospitable land near where her mother lives. Another man joins her in watching the animals, and then says, 'Doesn't it give you hope?'

She asks what he means.

'Isn't it a relief that there're still things like that, a real bit of Old England still left, despite all these immigrants coming in?'

Richard Smyth, who repeats that anecdote, argues that similar attitudes manifest themselves surprisingly often within nature writing. He points out that *Tarka the Otter* — recently voted 'the UK's favourite nature book' — was written by Henry Williamson, a Hitler supporter and member of Mosley's British Union, whose naturalism developed in parallel to his fascism.[4]

In Germany in particular, right-wing Romanticism gloried in the hierarchy of the wilderness, contrasting the natural struggle for survival with the egalitarian decadence of cities. The contemporary anti-fascist Alexander Reid Ross points out that the word 'ecology' was coined by Ernst Haeckel, an influential race theorist, while 'biocentrism' was associated with the philosopher Ludwig Klages, who blamed environmental destruction on modernity ... and Jews.[5]

Such ideas found their way into National Socialism and its concept of 'Blood and Soil', the supposed biological basis of German nationalism. Nazi theorists such as Richard Walther Darré asserted a semi-mystical link between the German peasantry and the land on which they toiled. Deracinated cosmopolitans might thrive in the metropolis, but Aryans, the Nazis claimed, could only flourish with sufficient *lebensraum* (living space).

'There is no nationalism without environmentalism,' writes Person X, 'the natural environment of our lands shaped us just as we shaped it. We were born from our lands and our own culture was molded by these same lands. The protection and preservation of these lands is of the same importance as the protection and preservation of our own ideals and beliefs.'[6]

All of this comes straight from Nazism.

Today, the mainstream environmental movement identifies, for the most part, with the left. Yet a small but vocal eco-fascist tendency still exists, particularly online, where it posts, as Sarah Manavis puts it, 'a bespoke cocktail of alt-right memes, pictures of forests and cabins, hatred towards Jews, and rants about animal rights'.[7]

In his manifesto, Person X rehearses similar ideas. He denounces left-wing environmentalism, and blames the destruction of nature on immigration.

'The Europe of the future is not one of concrete and steel, smog and wires but a place of forests, lakes, mountains and meadows,' he tells us.

Once again, though, the curiously elevated language suggests a tension, with the forests, lakes, mountains, and meadows positioned rather oddly alongside an online aesthetic developed by the basement-dwelling computer nerds of 4chan and 8chan.

The disconnect between Person X's vision and his audience reflects the innate contradictions of fascist environmentalism. Hitler promised a mystical communion with the soil, but he delivered massive industrialisation in the construction of a war economy. The Aryan utopia that Person X lauds — those images of white mothers raising their white babies in idyllic rural settings

— pertains more to JRR Tolkien's *The Hobbit* than the twenty-first century fascist milieu of lulz, skinheads, and shitposts.

To understand the function of ecology within Person X's broader program, it's helpful to examine what he describes as his 'tactics for victory' — in particular, something he calls 'accelerationism'.

Robin MacKay and Armen Avanessian define accelerationism as 'the insistence that the only radical political response to capitalism is not to protest, disrupt, or critique, nor to await its demise at the hands of its own contradictions, but to accelerate its uprooting, alienating, decoding, abstractive tendencies'.[8]

Accelerationism grew from various left-wing sources: Marx's appreciation, in the *Communist Manifesto* and elsewhere, of the dynamism of the market; certain passages from Lenin suggesting that revolutionaries should 'support, accelerate, facilitate' the development of social contradictions; and the poststructuralist enthusiasm of Deleuze, Guattari, and Lyotard for the libidinal energy of late capitalism.

But most accounts of the movement focus, in particular, on the British philosopher Nick Land and the Cybernetic Culture Research Unit that he headed in Warwick University for a brief period in the mid-nineties. Rejecting what they saw as the miserablism of the contemporary left, Land argued that the only way to escape the logic of capitalism was, as Benjamin Noys says, to 'take it further, to follow its lines of flight or deterritorialisation, to speed-up beyond the limits of production and so to rupture the limit of capital itself'.[9]

The CCRU duly gloried in electronic music, the novels of William Gibson and HP Lovecraft, automation, technology, amphetamines, and the imminent destruction of liberal-humanist norms. Eventually, Land suffered a mental collapse ('his work increasingly defied comprehension, sometimes departing from language altogether in favor of invented alphabets and number systems'), fled academia, and then moved to China, where his writing became authoritarian and explicitly racist.

Over time, 'accelerationism' found a new audience as part of the so-called Dark Enlightenment, a gaggle of writers combining Silicon Valley libertarianism with corporatism. They saw the economic and political tendencies that particularly worried liberals (such as the dysfunctionality of parliamentary democracy, the influence of multinationals, and the growing dominance of AI and high technology) as seeds to be nourished — embryonic of a new, anti-egalitarian order.

Matthew N. Lyons argues that Person X's manifesto owes less to Land than to discussions about terrorism on the neo-Nazi forum 'Iron March' and, in particular, in William Pierce's novel *The Turner Diaries*, a book that lays out a blueprint for a fascist revolution through terrorism.[10]

Certainly, Person X's embrace of accelerationism means, above all, an advocacy of social and political breakdown as both necessary and desirable. Stability and comfort constitute, he says, major obstacles to the fascist revolution, which can only arise from 'the great crucible of crisis'. As a result, fascists 'must destabilize and discomfort society where ever possible'. Even someone pushing for minimal changes with which fascists might agree should be considered 'useless or even damaging': far better, Person X says, to have 'radical, violent change regardless of its origins'.

To this end, he advocates 'actions such as voting for political candidates that radically change or challenge entrenched systems, radicalising public discourse by both supporting, attacking, vilifying, radicalising and exaggerating all societal conflicts and attacking or even assassinating weak or less radical leaders/influencers on either side of social conflicts'.[11]

Yet, if Person X draws on Pierce, his argument also recalls another common source of accelerationist thought: the poet and fascist theorist Filippo Marinetti.

In his *Futurist Manifesto* of 1909, Marinetti declared speed 'a new form of beauty', one that should be celebrated like the machine age that birthed it. His love of technology was accompanied by a distinctively fascist glorification of 'aggressive action, a feverish insomnia, the racer's stride the mortal leap, the punch and the slap'.[12]

For Marinetti, the exemplary form of 'aggressive action' was, of course, war:

War is beautiful because it enriches a flowering meadow with the fiery orchids of machine guns. War is beautiful because it combines the gunfire, the cannonades, the cease-fire, the scents, and the stench of putrefaction into a symphony. War is beautiful because it creates new architecture, like that of the big tanks, the geometrical formation flights, the smoke spirals from burning villages, and many others.[13]

His enthusiasm for violence contains more than a whiff of the rage-killer's exultation — the same sensual satisfaction in destruction, the same idealisation of the power inherent in slaughter. Just as the autogenic gunman often ended his rampage by shooting himself, the annihilation Marinetti celebrated was also a self-annihilation. As Walter Benjamin famously noted, the Futurist enjoyment of war amounted to an alienated humanity experiencing 'its own destruction as an aesthetic pleasure of the first order'.[14]

Noys makes the same point about accelerationism in the 1990s: it seemed attractive because it turned the seeming inevitability of capitalism into something desirable, even liberating. Defeat became victory — a victory 'registered in the form of ecstatic suffering'.

The argument provides the basis for a deeper understanding of Person X's eco-fascism. On the surface, his accelerationism contradicts his environmentalism.

'Hurrah! No more contact with the vile earth!' shouted Marinetti. The slogan does not seem much of a basis for a concern about ecology.

Yet right-wing trends within environmentalism invariably draw upon the ideas of the English parson Thomas Malthus. In 1798, Malthus published his *Essay on the Principle of Population*, in which he identified a supposed tendency for the (exponential) growth of human fertility to outstrip the (linear) growth of subsistence.

Malthus himself was primarily an opponent of the poor laws, penning his tract to decry early schemes for the provision of welfare, which, he claimed, would merely encourage the destitute to breed. His ideas were, however, taken up by many ecologists, who associated the destruction of wilderness with the growth of the human population.

But any political campaign against overpopulation inevitably raised the question as to which particular people constituted the problem — and that was something for which fascists always had an answer.

Sarah Manavis explains it:

[A] Malthusian take on the impact of population growth underpins almost the entirety of eco-fascism. Many eco-fascists are also eugenicists, who believe that a culling of the population, and specific races within that population, is the only way to ensure that the planet survives. While not all eco-fascists go as far as supporting mass murder, most hold that immigration has caused overpopulation in their countries and insists that the only solution is to deport those they deem non-indigenous.[15]

This is precisely the perspective of Person X. He denounces 'the left' for both 'controlling all discussion regarding environmental preservation' and for 'presiding over the continued destruction of the natural environment itself through mass immigration and uncontrolled urbanization'.

He then explains, with horrific bluntness, the fascist 'solution' to the environmental crisis: 'Kill the invaders, kill the overpopulation and by doing so save the environment.'[16] Person X's environmentalism centres less on preservation than on destruction.

In theory, eco-fascism celebrates 'forests, lakes, mountains, and meadows'; in practice, it demands the murder of leftists and ethnic minorities.

If his manifesto leaves the goals of eco-fascism hazy and amorphous, it presents its strategic imperatives with a brutal clarity. Person X enthuses about a future of Aryan villages nestled in the wilderness — but right now, he wants to kill and destroy.

For progressives, environmentalism means slowing down or stopping climate change. Person X presents a quite different perspective. For him, global warming constitutes a problem for which it is itself the answer, bringing about the destabilisation he wants. He welcomes catastrophic social breakdown: that is what his accelerationism means.

The writer Umair Haque has noted the compatibility between climate denialism and contemporary fascism.

> [C]atastrophic climate change is not a problem for fascists, it is a solution. History's most perfect, lethal, and efficient one means of genocide, ever, period. Who needs to build a camp or a gas chamber when the flood and hurricane will do the dirty work for free? ... [C]limate change accords perfectly with the foundational fascist belief that only the strong should survive, and the weak — the dirty, the impure, the foul — should perish.[17]

Paradoxically, the same argument explains Person X's eco-fascism, a doctrine in which fascism dominates ecology. 'Why focus on immigration and birth rates when climate change is such a huge issue?' Person X asks himself. He answers. 'Because they are the same issue, the environment is being destroyed by over population.'[18]

In other words, climate change justifies doing nothing about climate change, since, for Person X, it's always and only the birth rates that matter. Or, more exactly, climate change justifies mass murder and ethnic cleansing as the only 'solutions' to the environmental emergency.

Person X's 'environmentalism' doesn't represent a moderation of his platform. It is part of his accelerationism, the basis for an intensification of fascist violence. Fascists, he says, 'must destabilize and discomfort society' — and what destabilises and discomforts society more than climate change?

The result is a position paradoxically compatible with the era, given that it welcomes 'the great crucible of crisis'. As industrial civilisation hurtles down the tracks of catastrophic ecological breakdown, mainstream environmentalists pull weakly on the emergency break. Person X, however, calls for more speed to the engine.

'Do not fear change,' he advises his followers, 'we are change.'[19]

Once again, the slogan recalls the proto-Nazi Freikorps and their cry, 'We ourselves are the War.'

That comparison should give us pause. Person X presents a systematised manifesto calling for racist terror in the name of a social disruption he thinks will culminate in ethnic cleansing and genocide.

It's an evil program, the wickedness of which is not diminished by its self-evident impossibility. But impossible programs still attract followers, irrespective of their wickedness. The permanent combat sought by the Freikorps wasn't, in any conventional sense, achievable — but that didn't prevent the first supporters of Adolf Hitler from devoting themselves to it.

6
'COBBERS'
AUSTRALIA AND THE FASCIST MILIEU

Person X's interactions with the Australian fascist movement provide a context for assessing the threat his project poses. Though he made contact with — and donated to — fascist groups around the world, he saw the relatively small movement in his native Australia as particularly important. On social media, he used as his avatar the 'Aussie shitposter meme', an image popularised by a group of Australian alt-right podcasters known as the 'Dingoes'. Before he embarked on his murder spree, he thanked his associates on 8chan, using the archaic Australianism 'cobbers'.[1]

He participated regularly in debates on the (now deleted) Facebook pages of the United Patriots Front and the True Blue Crew, two tiny Australian fascist groups. That was why the UPF activist Tom Sewell acknowledged that Person X had 'been on the scene for a while'.[2]

The events of 9/11 altered the terrain for far-right politics in Australia particularly sharply, since they took place only a few weeks after the arrival of the Norwegian freighter MV *Tampa*.

The *Tampa* carried a cargo of 433 refugees — members of the Afghan Hazara minority, rescued from a sinking fishing boat — and its presence in Australian waters only two months out from an election provided a key talking point for John Howard and his unpopular conservative government, a message that quickly became entwined with 9/11. Two days after the attacks on New York, defence minister Peter Reith was warning that refugee boats could 'be a pipeline for terrorists to come in and use your country as a staging post for terrorist activities'.[3] Howard duly staged a remarkable comeback.

The Islamophobia arising from the Australian commitment to the Afghan and Iraq invasions (and the War on Terror more generally) fused with anti-refugee sentiment, as the major parties competed to 'stop the boats'.

Again, the post-9/11 racial discourse eventually facilitated the rise of an outsider anti-elitism, exemplified by the return of Pauline Hanson. Hanson had come to prominence in the mid-nineties by injecting traditional racist themes into public life, particularly the threat of a supposed 'Asian invasion', before her One Nation party collapsed acrimoniously in the 2000s.

In the 1990s, Hanson had never mentioned Islam. In 2015, she transitioned from old-fashioned racism to the more modern kind. She returned to politics proposing a ban on 'Muslim immigration' and on the construction of mosques, and calling for a royal commission into Islam. On that basis, One Nation won four Senate seats.

During her comeback 'Fed Up' tour, Pauline Hanson spoke at an anti-Islam rally in Rockhampton hosted by Reclaim Australia, an organisation reminiscent of European Islamophobic groups such as Pegida. Reclaim Australia presented itself as ordinary 'mums and dads' organising on Facebook to express their outrage about terrorism, particularly the Lindt café terrorist siege (in which a lone gunman, Man Haron Monis, had held hostage ten customers and murdered two of them).[4]

Even though RA was, like Hanson herself, right-wing populist rather than fascist, fascist activists played a role in the marches it organised throughout 2015.[5]

In May, a Cooma-based sanitation worker, Shermon Burgess, denounced other Reclaim Australia activists as 'traitors' and declared the need for a new group. Burgess had previously been associated with the fascist grouplet the Australian Defence League.[6] As singer and songwriter in the band Eureka Brigade, he'd presented his politics unambiguously, celebrating the 2005 race riots at Cronulla in New South Wales as 'Australia's Muslim Holocaust'.[7]

Since then, he had built a sizeable presence on Facebook and YouTube as 'The Great Aussie Patriot'. He used that profile to launch the United Patriots Front, in alliance with a small coterie of activists from the fascist right, as well as (briefly) the religious Islamophobes of the Catch The Fire Ministries/Rise Up Australia Party.[8]

One of the UPF's prominent members was Neil Erikson, a man with a long history on the far right — he later told a journalist he'd become a neo-Nazi at the age of 16.[9] In 2015, he had pleaded guilty to stalking a Melbourne rabbi. 'Give me the money, Jew, or else I will get you,' he had said to Rabbi Dovid Gutnick, abusing him for his religion over multiple phone calls.[10]

Like Burgess, Erikson regularly delivered YouTube lectures, posting them on the multiple Facebook pages he hosted.

Burgess's other key recruit, the Melbourne-based carpenter and amateur bodybuilder Blair Cottrell, was more ideological. An avowed Hitlerite, Cottrell believed every school classroom should feature a picture of the Nazi leader.[11] In the early phases of the UPF, Cottrell contributed on-camera lectures in fascist theory he called 'Philosophical Re-education', clips in which he railed against 'diversity', 'egalitarianism', and similar notions.[12]

Like Person X, the UPF decided pragmatically to promote Islamophobia. In one private Facebook conversation screenshotted by the anti-fascist activist Andy

Fleming, Erikson chatted with Cottrell about how to balance various bigotries.

'My personal opinion is stick to the Muslim shit and Cultural Marxism for max support,' Erikson said. '[D]o Jews later you don't need to show your full hand.'

Cottrell concurred: 'Yeah good advice and that's my current attitude as well. It will take years to prepare for the Jewish problem. If any of us came out with it now we would be slaughtered by public opinion.'[13]

Yet, despite courting the mainstream, the main UPF leaders barely disguised their commitment to the violence so central to fascism. At various times, both Erikson and Cottrell celebrated the eradication of those they deemed enemies.

In 2007, a fascist named Josué Estébanez stabbed Carlos Palomino, a 16-year-old anti-racist activist, on a Madrid train carriage. The crime was captured on video — and so Estébanez became a cult figure for the fascist right. (Symptomatically, Person X inscribed the name 'Estébanez' on one of the rifles he used in Christchurch.)[14]

In July 2015, Neil Erikson posted footage of Palomino's murder to advertise a UPF rally. Narrating the action, he described the attack as 'gold' and 'bloody awesome' — and then exulted in the passengers' fear.

'Look they're like ants running away from one patriot,' he said. 'We have the power. There he is by himself, he won the battle. One patriot versus a thousand left wing unwashed scum. Bring on July 18, Melbourne, Parliament House, 1pm.'

Erikson later told journalists his video had been 'doctored', though he produced no evidence for his claim.[15]

Then, after the murder of Heather Heyer during the Unite the Right rally in Charlottesville, Virginia, Erikson posted the mugshot of Heyer's killer, framing the image with smiling emojis with love hearts for eyes.[16]

As for Cottrell, he explained on social media how anti-fascists would be 'executed post revolution or sent to labour camps, along with all the liberal leaders'.[17]

'If I am ever in the appropriate position of power,' he tweeted, on another occasion, 'I will deport the enemies of my country and execute those who refuse to go. Laugh if you want but when the time comes I will campaign with that as my slogan, and I will win.'[18]

The internet proved a tremendously important resource for the far right in Australia, not least because it allowed activists to relate to developments overseas.

The Dingoes, the group from whom Person X borrowed his avatar, began producing a podcast called The Convict Report in 2016. It was hosted by the Right Stuff media hub, alongside the fascist *Daily Shoah* podcast of Mike Enoch (whom the Dingoes sought to bring to Australia).[19] When the Dingoes launched their online presence, they described themselves as '#AltRight, but not in the way that violates #Rule1' — a reference to the rules of 4chan.[20]

Despite adorning their website with the Nazi '88' symbol, the Dingoes convinced Federal MP George Christensen and former Labor leader Mark Latham to appear on their podcast.[21]

The internet allowed Australian fascists to link up with their domestic supporters in a geographically huge but sparsely populated country. Through Facebook, Shermon Burgess could initiate a national organisation from a regional town in southern New South Wales — and Person X could participate in that movement from Grafton, 1,000 kilometres away.

In late 2015, internal tensions erupted in the UPF, with Cottrell deposing Burgess from the leadership. Erikson sided with Burgess (releasing videos exposing the Nazi past of various UPF figures), before eventually reuniting with Cottrell.[22]

Person X followed the schism closely, intervening on Facebook to denounce Erikson and Burgess as 'useful idiots'.

'Leave the nationalist leadership to Blair ... or be named obvious plants and traitors,' Person X warned.

He repeatedly posted endorsements of Cottrell, a man he hailed as his 'Emperor'. When Cottrell appeared on television, Person X could barely contain his glee.

'Never believed we would have a true leader of

the nationalist movement in Australia,' he wrote, 'and especially not so early in the game. Would gladly stand behind you.'[23]

Person X's enthusiasm for Cottrell makes sense given that they shared the view that 'enemies' should be executed. In his manifesto, Person X threatens anti-fascists directly, saying, 'I want your neck under my boot.'[24]

On a comment on the UPF Facebook page, he made the same point.

'Communists will get what communists get,' he wrote. 'I would love to be there holding one end of the rope when you get yours traitor.'[25]

He repeated the sentiment in a Facebook Messenger conversation with an interlocutor, where he defended the UPF as 'the leading ethno-nationalist group within Australia'.

The conversation ended with Person X noting that the critic had been marked. '[I]f you are a Marxist,' he said, 'I hope you one day meet the rope.'

Though the police were warned, they did nothing, advising the complainant to use the block facility.

To the authorities, Person X's interventions probably seemed unexceptional because the UPF Facebook page was flooded with similar comments: calls for the bashings of leftists, the execution of journalists, the drowning of refugees, and so on.

'[T]here is,' wrote *The Saturday Paper*'s Martin McKenzie-Murray, 'a fondness in the patriot movement for the language of epidemiology — filth, disease, contamination. The popular metaphor is of a healthy body threatened by foreign bacteria. It is the language of battle. Extinction.'[26]

In some ways, the UPF resembled the Traditionalist Worker Party, in that, throughout 2015 and 2016, it organised real-world rallies and events, promising to (in Cottrell's words) unleash 'force and terror' against its opponents.[27]

Yet, like their overseas equivalents, the Australian fascists always reached many more people on social media than they did at demonstrations. At its peak, the UPF page gathered more than 120,000 likes, with individual Facebook posts generating hundreds of comments. The organisation — and its leaders — produced a stream of popular YouTube videos.

The vast majority of people who interacted with the Australian 'patriot movement' thus did so — like Person X — online. Yet leading activists repeatedly signalled that their ideas should be applied to the real world, particularly through real-world confrontations with those identified as enemies.

Neil Erikson, an inveterate attention-seeker, infamously confronted and racially abused then-Labor senator Sam Dastyari at a Melbourne pub, brought a coffin into a Moreland council meeting, and interrupted services at a Gosford church.[28]

In November 2015, Erikson, Cottrell, and two other UPF members made uninvited visits to the Melbourne Anarchist Club in Northcote and the left-wing community radio station 3CR. They entered both buildings and filmed those inside, with the footage later appearing online.[29]

The visits were clearly intimidatory, signalling to the UPF's enemies that their location was known. That intimidation was exacerbated by Cottrell's own history of criminal stalking. He had been jailed in 2013 for arson, burglary, and damaging property belonging to a romantic rival. In a prison video, he discussed how he'd waited outside the man's house with knives stashed in his jacket.[30]

Even more alarmingly, on the MAC visit, Cottrell had been accompanied by a UPF activist called Chris Shortis. *The Age* later revealed Shortis's social media history, including clips in which he declared himself a 'Biblical crusader' and a 'gun lover', and images in which he posed bare-chested clutching high-powered rifles and pistols. Shortis denounced Islam as 'demonic', and claimed the UN intended to install the Pope to head up a new world order. He insisted that, eventually, 'patriots' would find it necessary to take up arms against both Muslims and the Australian government.

'We'll end up fighting [Muslims] one way or another
...' he said in one video, 'we should be doing it with
absolute brutality.'

The University of South Australia academic Chloe
Patton made the obvious comparison: 'Here we have an
individual who is clearly radicalised, who is brandishing
firearms while preaching holy war. The intricate conspiracy theories and crusader symbolism immediately brings
to mind Anders Breivik.'[31]

If the strategy of the UPF mirrored that of the
American fascists, so too did its eventual fate.

In August and October 2015, the UPF attended two
anti-Muslim protests in the regional city of Bendigo that
attracted hundreds of supporters. Thereafter, it found
itself consistently outnumbered by anti-racist activists
and police, so much so that its events became increasingly unviable.

In early 2016, Cottrell announced the launch of a
parliamentary party under the unlikely name 'Fortitude',
but proved unable to gather the necessary signatures
for its registration. As the UPF members bickered and
threatened each other, Cottrell, Shortis, and Erikson
were found guilty of inciting contempt against Muslims
with a video showing a fake beheading.[32] Shortis was
then stripped of his gun licence.[33]

At one point, Cottrell had explained to journalists the
centrality of Facebook to UPF. 'It's ... indispensable to

the development of our organisation,' he said. 'Without it, we would probably be a separatist cult where no one would be able to relate to us because no one would be able to actually hear us directly ...'[34]

So it proved. In mid-2017, the page was deleted (perhaps after an intervention by security agencies)[35] in a final blow to the already disintegrating organisation.[36]

Thereafter, key UPF members went through a reassessment process reminiscent of the American 'Optics War'. Cottrell, Sewell, and others abandoned their attempt to build an overtly political organisation. They established, with the help of James Buckle (a former president of Firearm Owners United), The Lads Society: a project based around martial-arts and bodybuilding gyms.[37]

Like Anglin, they didn't believe they were ready for further confrontations. Where Anglin wanted to build cadres online, the TLS wanted to recruit in their gymnasiums, rather than at marches at which they were outnumbered and harassed.

'We tried many things in the past, but this project is different,' said Sewell. 'We want to provide a space for people like us.'[38]

That was the context in which he, on behalf of the TLS, contacted Person X via Facebook and invited him to join. According to Sewell, Person X refused, partly because he was about to leave for New Zealand — but also because he no longer cared about optics.

The activists associated with the UPF/TLS thus parted company with Person X. They played no part in his terror attack, which they subsequently condemned.

But they hadn't shed their own fascist ideas. Indeed, the personnel of The Lads Society overlapped with that of Antipodean Resistance, an openly Nazi organisation.[39] As Sewell made clear in a discussion with *The Age*, the TLS members still wanted to build a white ethno-state, and they were still prepared to fight against those who opposed them.

'I'm not going to give you any explicit threat,' Sewell told the journalist, 'but it's pretty f--king obvious what's going to happen [if they faced opposition]' — and then added that his enemies 'had names and addresses'.[40]

The statement, so redolent of the UPF's approach, highlighted the opportunities that even the small Australian scene presented for Person X's strategy.

One of the 'names and addresses' identified by the UPF during its brief lifespan belonged, as we have seen, to the Melbourne Anarchist Club. In 2016, police charged Phil Galea, a heavyset, wild-bearded man from Braybook, with plotting to blow up the MAC.[41]

During Galea's committal hearing on charges of planning to commit a terrorist act and collecting material in connection with a terrorist act, the prosecution referred to phone taps. These intercepts allegedly showed Galea deciding to bomb the Trades Hall in Carlton and a building belonging to the socialist group Resistance. He was also said to be targeting the same Melbourne Anarchist Club that Cottrell, Erikson, and Shortis had blamed for housing their enemies.[42]

Had the bombings gone ahead, the results would have been catastrophic, as Galea seemed to understand.

A witness called Darren Norsworth said that Galea considered the bystanders who would have been killed by his attacks as 'casualties of war'. Galea was said to have been assembling a manual (something he called the 'Patriots Cook Book') to train right-wingers in techniques of violence.

'One of the things he had [in his purported manual],' explained Norsworth, 'was how much battery acid to inject into a leftie. He thought it was important to show the right wing how to hurt the left.'[43]

Another witness, Heidi Martin, said Galea discussed 'torture techniques' and 'chopping people up'.[44]

Galea did not seem to have been in contact with Person X. He had, however, been connected to Reclaim Australia. Even though some of his associates described him as 'nuts', he had served as an administrator for some of RA's social media. He'd also been a supporter of the True Blue Crew, another tiny fascist group — and one that Person X had explicitly praised.[45]

After Galea's arrest, the TBC leader, Kane Miller, angrily rejected any association with his plans. 'Anyone to think an act of terrorism,' he said, 'or to hurt innocent people is the right way to go about either fixing things or creating awareness is an absolute idiot.'

Miller played no role in Galea's bomb-making schemes, just as he played no role in Person X's massacre. Yet Miller — like Galea, the UPF, and Person X saw physical violence as key to defeating the enemies of fascists.

'How do we fucking do it, TBC?' Kane had screamed to his supporters during one rally.

'Smash cunts!' came the reply.[46]

Galea had clearly agreed. After escaping incarceration on an earlier weapons charge, Galea had posted to Facebook an image of man wearing a TBC patch swinging a pole to hit counter-protesters. The accompanying text read: 'TBC cleaning Australia: one leftie at a time.'[47]

The tiny fascist scene in Australia has always attracted criminals, including a number of murderers. As recently as 2016, three members of the Perth Nazi group Aryan Nations bashed to death a fourth person in an attempt to secure an insurance payout.[48]

But, as Person X understood, such criminality became particularly dangerous because of its association with ideology. The commitment to redemptive violence against perceived enemies, combined with the dissociative effects of the internet, created an environment in which atrocities could be normalised, especially for young men who were already mentally troubled.

Obviously, 'smashing cunts' was not the same as setting off bombs (or shooting up a mosque). But the exterminism that ran through the 'patriot movement' meant that the difference could seem to be one of tactics rather than of principles.

In a political culture in which leading figures repeatedly praised the execution or murder of opponents, individuals planning horrific acts could find solace and encouragement.

Again, the prominent members of the organised fascist groups in Australia rejected Person X's strategy, both before his murders and after them. But Person X was not reliant on prominent figures within organisations. His approach was calculated to appeal to the marginal and the unstable, who, via the internet, could easily latch onto fascism and the violence it encouraged.

In 2017, a neo-Nazi called Michael James Holt was sent to jail in New South Wales for the possession of child pornography and a huge arsenal of real and replica weapons.[49] Holt had previously told a school counsellor that he regarded Adolf Hitler as 'the greatest person to live', and said that he often fantasised about committing mass homicides. When they raided his house, police found eight firearms hidden in cupboards, as well as a huge stash of fascist literature. The judge mused that Holt had the potential to be 'the next Martin Bryant' (a reference to the man who murdered 35 people in Port Arthur, Tasmania, in 1996).[50]

Holt seems to have been aligned with the Christian Separatist Church, an American far-right organisation, rather than any of the local grouplets. Yet he knew at least some of the UPF leaders online.

In a series of posts on Facebook, Holt had documented his deteriorating mental health, writing 'I am going crazy at a rapidly increasing rate' and 'what tha [sic] fuck's going on get back to me somebody, need to stomp some skulls'. He added, 'Need to shed some fuckin' commie blood, if there isn't a rumble today we should fuckin start one', and then wrote, 'mudbloods are committing a crime just by encroaching the upon [sic] personal space of those of Noble Blood, the punishment for which should be death!'

Those last two messages — explicit calls for political violence by a clearly disturbed young man — were both 'liked' by Neil Erikson.[51]

Every political movement attracts fringe elements. But the nature of fascism meant that truly dangerous people were not deterred but encouraged. It is difficult, after all, to think of another milieu in which a leading activist might express public approval for a post about racial murder.

The Australian fascist scene in which Person X intervened in 2015 and 2016 was noisy but not particularly large by historical or international standards. Much bigger movements existed in many countries.

In any case, the repercussions of Christchurch were felt globally, as Person X knew they would be. There were young men like Michael Holt all over the world. They didn't need to go to fascist meetings to stumble upon Person X's manifesto and video. Once they found them, they would be presented both with a cause and a method of serving that cause.

Imitators might come from anywhere.

CONCLUSION

HOPE AGAINST HATE

The atrocities committed by Person X will not lead to the establishment of a fascist dictatorship in New Zealand or anywhere else. In that specific sense — in his conviction that he will be freed like Nelson Mandela by the victory of 'his people' — Person X might be described as delusional. But there was nothing delusional in his belief that he would encourage imitative crimes.

In the immediate aftermath of the killings, rival far-right leaders (including Blair Cottrell) worried that the violence would hurt their cause.[1] But others — particularly those attuned to the online environment — were more enthusiastic.

'Even though it is bad behavior, it definitely feels really fucking good to watch,' wrote Andrew 'weev' Auernheimer on *The Daily Stormer.*

His co-thinker, Andrew Anglin, agreed.

'Of the mass shootings I have seen, this is by far the funniest one of them all.' While claiming not to support the massacre, he added, significantly, 'it sure as hell wasn't bad optics.'[2]

Identifying himself as a veteran of the 'Optics War', the far-right commentator Travis LeBlanc expressed astonishment at the response to Person X's actions.

'There's something ... different about this. Like something has changed, like a corner has been turned ... This Christchurch massacre has done something that other public relations catastrophes such as Dylann Roof and Charlottesville did not do: it has actually sparked a dialogue favorable to our cause.'[3]

On fascist-inflected sites like Gab or 8chan, Person X's ability to read his audience has become apparent, with many commentators using his name or image as an avatar. Others spoke admiringly of what *The Daily Stormer* called the 'mosque prank'.

Anons might praise the massacre, or decry it as a false-flag operation carried out by Jews (sometimes both at the same time), but they remain fascinated by it. As one anon exclaimed, Person X produced 'possibly the most powerful meme we have ever had: the shooting video'.[4]

The memification of Christchurch might best be illustrated by the reports published in multiple media outlets in June 2019 about a first-person shooter game that allowed users to play as Person X, whom it described as a man 'who turned his back on a life of eternal shitposting and decided to become an Epic Gamer'.[5]

The overwhelming tenor of the coverage was, quite properly, horror and disgust at the trivialisation of mass murder. Yet condemnation by the mainstream media wasn't perceived by the fascists as a setback. They had, in fact, deliberately set out to attract it, with an 8chan user boasting about making the game — and urging fellow anons to report it.

'Identify yourself as a concerned parent and Navy Seal,' he said, 'and say you found it on reddit.'

He knew — as did his readers — that normie disapproval would delight the intended audience of the prank: the young 8channers for whom public outrage was as amusing as the game itself. Some of them, he hoped, might start brooding on what imitating Person X might be like.

The incident, trivial in itself, illustrated some of the difficulties in responding to the Christchurch massacre and the new fascism more generally.

Immediately after the mosque shooting, considerable attention focused on the media and its responsibilities in covering such attacks. Many progressive journalists and critics argued for the adoption of protocols similar to those developed by No Notoriety, an advocacy group formed by Tom and Caren Teves after the murder of their son Alex during a rage massacre in Colorado.[6] New Zealand Prime Minister Jacinda Ardern advocated a plan dubbed the 'Christchurch Call', intended to create a framework for the media to report on massacres and other atrocities without boosting them.[7]

In an extensive analysis of Christchurch coverage, the *Columbia Journalism Review* suggested that 'best practice' for the media included not publishing the shooter's name, the title or contents of his manifesto, the name of the forum on which he posted his document, or any specific memes he deployed.

'Don't describe or detail the shooter's ideology,' it implored.[8]

Along similar lines, journalism academic Denis Muller criticised *The Australian* for providing Person X with a 'propaganda victory' by publishing extracts from his writing.

'It is enough to know,' Muller argued, 'that the manifesto suggests the terrorist was radicalised during his travels in Europe and seemed determined to take revenge for atrocities committed there by Islamist terrorists.'[9]

But these arguments, while well meaning, are not persuasive. Knowing that Person X was 'radicalised' in Europe was manifestly not enough, since it explained very little about his action. Person X was not simply someone taking 'revenge' against Islamist terrorists. He was ideologically committed to fascism, a movement that is consistently handed propaganda victories by a mass media unwilling or incapable of understanding it.

This is perhaps clearest in respect of the United Patriots Front, the organisation that Person X so admired. Elements of the Australian media helped boost the UPF during that organisation's lifespan — not because they described its ideology, but precisely because they didn't.

In 2016, the government youth radio station Triple J featured Blair Cottrell on a panel about 'patriotism' (and then, in 2017, invited neo-Nazi Eli Mosley to discuss the Charlottesville protest, in a segment then trolled by alt-righters pretending to be Jewish).[10] The next year, Sky News featured Cottrell discoursing on immigration in a one-on-one interview with Adam Giles.[11]

When the UPF and the TBC organised a meeting to plan vigilante responses to 'African gangs', Channel Seven boasted of being 'granted exclusive access'.

'[T]hey call themselves patriots,' the reporter told the camera, 'and say they have come together to help average Australians deal with what they are calling an immigrant crime crisis … Take a listen to what their leaders tonight had to say.'

The station then broadcast Blair Cottrell and Kane Miller — without disclosing that the two men opining about crime were themselves criminals.[12]

In response to criticism, conservative journalists warned against censorship. But that missed the point. The problem wasn't that the media had provided too much information about the UPF, but rather that it had failed to provide enough. The glaring absence was an explanation of the UPF's ideology — one that didn't resort to euphemisms such as 'far right' or 'nationalist', but instead discussed fascism and its historical and theoretical relationship with political violence. Had the nature of the UPF been established, journalists, like everyone else, would have been in a better position to discuss media strategies for the coverage of such an organisation.

If anything, the Christchurch killings have made the need for analysis more important, given the innate duplicity of the online fascist culture to which Person X belonged.[13]

Yet, in the wake of the massacre, Radio New Zealand, TVNZ, MediaWorks, Stuff, and *The New Zealand Herald* signed a statement agreeing not to quote Person X's document or other statements he made.[14]

No one could disagree with the need for sensitivity, given the horrendous suffering produced by the massacre. But many of the editorial decisions made in the wake of the killings were presented not as efforts to lessen the grief of relatives and friends, but as interventions to counter Person X politically.

Yet Person X did not want a mainstream audience for his manifesto and video. Both were coded specifically for reception by the fascist right on 8chan, Gab, and similar platforms — and, irrespective of the decisions made by the media, both circulated widely in those forums, where bans by the New Zealand state simply gave them more cachet.

The desire to avoid amplification of his rhetoric (while well intentioned) rested on a profoundly mistaken sense of his project. The power of Person X's manifesto stemmed from its complex relationship with its online audience rather than the deployment of any particular slogan.

Like all fascist programs, the document contains racist, populist, and conservative nostrums, stitched together by a commitment to horrific violence. A refusal to discuss Person X's ideas meant, in practice, a refusal to acknowledge how many of them were widely shared in the mainstream, including by major outlets. You did not need to search the dark web to find examples of Islamophobia; you could encounter anti-immigrant rhetoric on every TV station and in every tabloid, as well as in the statements of major politicians.

To take merely one example, in August 2018, Andrew Bolt, a popular columnist for the Murdoch press in Australia, published an article in the nation's biggest-selling tabloids explaining that 'immigration [was] becoming colonisation'. Beneath a headline warning about 'The foreign invasion', he explained that 'a tidal wave of immigrants [was sweeping] away what's left of our national identity'.[15]

The piece contrasted an implicitly white 'we' against Muslims, Chinese, Vietnamese, Cambodians, Indians, and other non-white ethnicities. '[W]e should resist this colonising of Australia,' Bolt said, 'while there is still an "us" that can.' It included, in a list of suburbs suffering from 'invasion', North Caulfield — and there Bolt complained, '41 per cent of residents are Jews ... Such colonising will increasingly be our future as we gain a critical mass of born-overseas migrants.'

Bolt did not call for violence or endorse terrorism. But the arguments in his piece, including the notion of Jewish colonisers, were common talking points among the fascist right.[16]

The dismissal of Person X's writings as ravings that need not or should not be discussed have disguised the disturbing familiarity of much of what he said. It has also done nothing to inoculate social media users against the online fascist presence.

In June 2019, *The New York Times* published a fascinating study of a young man called Caleb Cain, a shy college dropout from Appalachia who described himself as having fallen 'down the alt-right rabbit hole'. Using Cain's browsing history, it showed how YouTube, in particular, gradually steered him from conventional liberalism to alt-right and fascist content.

Cain discussed how he was initially attracted by right-wingers advocating free speech and attacking feminism — people making, in other words, arguments you could find on most conservative talk shows. Yet they portrayed themselves as truth-tellers, presenting facts that the humourless social-justice warriors (SJWs) in the mainstream wanted suppressed.

He became absorbed in the never-ending dramas of the YouTube community, in which his new conservative heroes battled a constant stream of SJW villains. By day, he worked packing boxes at a furniture warehouse — and in the evening, he fell asleep watching videos from his favourite creators.

As he absorbed more politically extreme material, he felt as if he'd joined an exclusive club, full of forbidden knowledge. 'I felt like I was chasing uncomfortable truths,' he said. 'I felt like it was giving me power and respect and authority.'[17]

In that description — and in his account of how he lost touch with his friends and family — you can faintly see the circumstances in which Person X's massacre script might exercise its sway. Cain depicted himself as someone increasingly aggrieved by the real world, and craving the power he associated with right-wing authoritarianism. Under different circumstances, such a person might, perhaps, have been induced to make 'a real life effort'.

Ardern's 'Christchurch Call' sought to prevent social media from enabling extremist content. But, in anticipation of such measures, many of the platforms had already sought — just as they had after Charlottesville — to purge the more notorious far-rightists employing their services.

In all probability, each new round of deletions from Twitter, Facebook, and YouTube did genuine damage to online fascism. Certainly, the UPF's loss of access to Facebook helped disrupt that organisation, while the post-Charlottesville exclusion of American leaders contributed to the chaos gripping the fascist movement after Unite the Right. The whining of Milo Yiannopoulos about his inability to use social media provided more anecdotal evidence that bans hindered the work of the alt-right.[18]

Yet, though Person X supported fascist organisations and ultimately wanted to build one, his strategy did not depend on their growth, nor did it require a high-profile spokesperson. Policing the isolated individuals attracted to lone-wolf terrorism thus posed more of a challenge than responding to prominent groups or ideologues.

Furthermore, an ecosystem of alternative options has already evolved, more or less explicitly to cater for those banned from Twitter and Facebook. Sites such as Gab might not deliver the same traffic as better-known platforms, but they do serve the same gateway function, introducing the curious browser to a huge array of fascists and white supremacists, in a setting where right-wingers feel no obligation whatsoever to moderate their views.

It would be naïve, in other words, to expect reforms of the major social media corporations to provide an answer to Christchurch. Such companies run as businesses rather than public utilities. Even if they can be shamed by political outrage, they're ultimately driven by the pursuit of profit — and the inflammatory accounts of the far right deliver user engagement that can be monetised via advertising.

For that reason, a thorough ban on fascist or far-right accounts seems unlikely.

The purges that have taken place have, in fact, been inconsistent and partial. In many cases, they have also targeted progressives, either because the relevant algorithm had somehow failed (as, for instance, when Twitter banned anti-fascist journalist David Neiwert because the book he promoted contained images of Ku Klux Klan hoods on its cover),[19] or because, rather than deleting fascists, moderators simply sought to shut down any content they deemed controversial. When, for instance, Facebook deleted some 800 pages and accounts for what it called 'spam and co-ordinated inauthentic behavior', *The Washington Post* noted that the groups affected included liberals as well as conservatives.[20]

By its nature, the moderation of social media remains undemocratic and unaccountable. The co-founder of Facebook, Chris Hughes, recently explained that Mark Zuckerberg exercised almost total power over the workings of that platform. 'Mark alone can decide how to configure Facebook's algorithms to determine what people see in their news feeds ... he sets the rules for how to distinguish violent and incendiary speech from the merely offensive,' he said.[21]

The dangers of relying on huge corporations to decide what material should or should not circulate should be, in the twenty-first century, entirely obvious.

It might be more useful, when thinking of strategies to counter online fascism, to draw analogies with what happened when the fascists in America (and Australia) tried to leverage their online popularity into real-world activism between 2015 and 2017.

The activism that pushed them back confirmed many of the lessons learned in opposition to Oswald Mosley in the 1940s and 1950s: namely, that public protests against fascist marches isolate and demoralise the cadres of the far right and discourage their new recruits. When Andrew Anglin warned his supporters not to attend the second Unite the Right protest, he said, 'We do not want the image of being a bunch of weird losers who march around like assholes while completely outnumbered and get mocked by the entire planet.'[22]

That was, indeed, very often the outcome, especially if the anti-fascist protests were broad-based and lively, and involved the local community. As Kim Kelly pointed out at the time, 'white nationalists, white supremacists, and other far-right hate groups' rally numbers are dwindling as the opposition to them grows broader and more militant'.[23]

The methodology might provide a basis for tackling fascism in the very different online context.

In his discussion with *The New York Times*, Caleb Cain explained how he became disaffected with the alt-right when he encountered progressives who 'spoke the native language of YouTube' and used the platform to effectively mock and debunk right-wing ideas.

Confronting the right remains much more difficult online than in the street, partly because fascists can congregate in all sorts of niches, and partly because the internet makes the sense of a collective real-world protest difficult to achieve. But Cain's experience suggests that progressives should continue developing new ways of campaigning online, to demonstrate that fascists remain 'weird losers and assholes' on the internet as well as off it, and to present alternatives to their hate.

At the same time, the struggle against fascism — both online and off — will always require determined combat against the bigotry on which fascists depend.

At the most obvious level, Islamophobia surely played a role in enabling Person X to escape state surveillance, despite his online engagement with the UPF and other fascist groups. For instance, had Person X been a young Muslim man who had, say, left more than 30 comments on a Facebook page belonging to Islamists on which death threats were made against white Australians, had he collected guns, and had he arrived unannounced at opponents' homes and businesses, one imagines he would have come to the attention of the relevant authorities — particularly after being reported to the police for threatening to kill someone.

The very ubiquity of anti-Islam sentiment provided, in a sense, cover for Person X. He did not stand out, simply because Islamophobia can be found almost everywhere.

What would happen if Islamophobia were rendered as taboo as anti-Semitism? With anti-Muslim and other forms of racism rendered as politically toxic as anti-Jewish sentiment, an immediate obstacle would be placed in the way of genuine fascists, who rely on 'acceptable' bigotry to make their program of extermination palatable.

But establishing a taboo on race-baiting would necessitate a confrontation with the various politicians and pundits who, without being fascists themselves, spread the ideas on which fascists rely.

As we have seen, contemporary racism draws much of its strength from policies that the major parties have supported for decades. Modern Islamophobia emerged from the war on terror, while anti-immigrant prejudice is reinforced by the infrastructure of exclusion that has been constructed in most developed countries.

In other words, many mainstream parties have now adapted to racist populism, as the 2016 US election showed. It should be remembered that, during the Republican primaries, the most serious challengers to Donald Trump came from his right, with other contenders trying to outdo him with their versions of Islamophobia and nativism. Whatever happens to Trump himself, Trumpism will remain central to the Republican Party for the foreseeable future.

Yet Trump's career also illustrates how the bond between mainstream conservatism and an outsider anti-elitism that shelters genuine fascists might be challenged.

In the wake of Unite the Right, the upsurge in anti-racist and anti-fascist organising blindsided Trump, and broke the links he had forged with the younger racist constituency organised by Bannon through *Breitbart*. The rift with 'Sloppy Steve' damaged the alt-right, but it also damaged Trump, who sunk to his lowest levels of popularity after Charlottesville.[24]

Similarly, the outrage following Person X's murders put renewed pressure on Australian fascists and on the politicians — such as Pauline Hanson's former associate Fraser Anning — who pandered to them. Prime Minister Scott Morrison was also pushed onto the defensive about the possibility that his party might preference Anning, and about his comments at a cabinet meeting in 2010 in which he allegedly urged his party to exploit Islamophobia for votes.[25]

'By attacking the right for its tendency towards authoritarianism,' argues David Renton, 'it is possible to sever the alliance between politicians of the centre right and the margins.'[26]

The ideas of the far right remain, after all, deeply unpopular, particularly when they are presented openly. Islamophobia might be widely tolerated, but very few normal people find notions of natural hierarchies and redemptive violence at all appealing, and so the mainstream right remains defensive about any association with fascists.

But in order to open up such rifts, anti-racists need to offer a real alternative, one that extends beyond critiques of the right. They need, more than anything, to offer hope.

In the first nineteen weeks of 2019, America saw fifteen school shootings in which someone was hurt or killed. These were not political crimes so much as acts of violence by disturbed individuals. Nevertheless, the proliferation of rage murders, particularly among the young, surely reflects a broader dysfunction, a social order deeply out of kilter.

In 2017, the American Psychological Association noted that climate change was producing widespread 'feelings of powerlessness, or exhaustion'.[27] Many of us feel that sentiment, given the seeming inevitability of environmental catastrophe. In some respects, the more you know, the worse you feel. Scientists and ecologists speak of the profound sadness that overcomes them when they read about the latest extinctions or the newest devastation.

In response to the recent Intergovernmental Panel on Climate Change report, the environmental activist Leo Murray tweeted, '[A]t times like this I feel a crushing weight of personal failure at how little I have achieved, and dread at the horrors ahead. I'm sorry. I'm trying.'[28]

But why try to prevent a catastrophe that many see as inevitable? With no clear path to a solution, conventional environmentalism can seem futile, even pathetic. Rather than seeking to douse the flames, why not fan them — or, better still, become the fire?

The agonising victory of accelerationism only becomes appealing when it's the only alternative to defeat. To truly fight fascism, we need to present something better. That need is urgent.

If Person X succeeds in recruiting an anonymous legion of imitators, many people will die. But his turn to terror stemmed from the inability of his cohort to build a viable fascist party — from, in other words, a political failure.

Other fascists might not fail. On the European continent, fascism already means something other than the tiny groups marching in Australia and the United States. In many countries there, fascists do march in the street. In some places, they even sit in parliament.

We are not facing a situation akin to Germany in 1933. Yet, for the first time in generations, a reprise of Germany in 1933 no longer seems completely ruled out.

As we've seen, fascism grows during crises, when a whole social layer, despairing at its prospects, embraces the idea of redemptive violence. In different circumstances, that violence needn't look as overtly nihilistic as a random massacre.

The British poet Michael Rosen once wrote of the assumption that 'fascism arrives in fancy dress/worn by grotesques and monsters'. This, he said, was wrong. As a mass phenomenon, fascism doesn't wear the face of a rage killer. It doesn't resemble Person X:

> Fascism arrives as your friend.
> It will restore your honour,
> make you feel proud,
> protect your house,
> give you a job,
> clean up the neighbourhood,
> remind you of how great you once were,
> clear out the venal and the corrupt,
> remove anything you feel is unlike you …[29]

We might also add to that list 'save the environment' since, throughout Europe, the far right increasingly talks about climate — and says the solution requires more borders and walls. With even progressives demanding the declaration of a 'climate emergency', it's not hard to imagine circumstances in which authoritarian 'emergency measures' enjoy wide support.

Rosen warns that fascists don't openly declare that they represent 'militias, mass/ imprisonments, transportations, war and/ persecution'. Yet that's a good description of the future that many commentators already predict if uncontrolled warming continues.

It doesn't have to be like that.

Naomi Klein argues that it's possible to think of climate change as not merely a threat but also as an opportunity, since any serious attempt to address the environmental crisis necessarily confronts many other social problems. The companies that pump pollutants into the environment simultaneously exploit their workforces; governments that clear forests also dispossess indigenous people.

'As part of the project of getting our emissions down to the levels many scientists recommend,' Klein says, 'we once again have the chance to advance policies that dramatically improve lives, close the gap between rich and poor, create huge numbers of good jobs, and reinvigorate democracy from the ground up.'[30]

In many places, a new generation now talks not merely of ameliorating climate change, but also of a program for green employment, sustainable transport, public housing, and new infrastructure. The fight against the forces ruining the planet means, they say, fighting for improvements, for change, for progress — a panoply of measures to make the future better, rather than simply less worse.

The more we offer an alternative to environmental destruction — and to the society that unleashes such destruction — the more squalid and miserable fascism seems.

And that, perhaps, is how victims of Christchurch might be commemorated.

We cannot undo what was done. We cannot restore to life Ansi Alibava, Husna Ahmed, Haji-Daoud Nabi, Sayyad Milne, or the others killed by fascist hate. But, by building a better world, we might yet do them honour.

Acknowledgements

This project was assisted by the Cultural Fund of the Copyright Agency. It relied, in particular, on the brave research and activism of Andy Fleming. The following people provided invaluable feedback: Geoff Boucher, Giovanni Tiso, and Stephanie Convery.

Notes

INTRODUCTION

1   Fergus Hunter, 'The Internet: optimised for hate, terror and chaos', *Sydney Morning Herald*, 16 March 2019.

2   Bill Bostock, Kieran Corcoran, and Bryan Logan, 'This Timeline of the Christchurch Mosque Terror Attacks Shows How New Zealand's Deadliest Shooting Unfolded', *Business Insider*, 19 March 2019.

3   'We Shall Speak Their Names: remembering the victims of the Christchurch mosque shootings', *The Guardian*, 21 March 2019.

4   Seth G Jones, 'The Rise of Far-Right Extremism in the United States', Center for Strategic and International Studies, 7 November 2018.

5   Anti Defamation League, 'Murder and Extremism in the United States in 2018', January 2019.

6   Andy Fleming, @slackbastard, 'Re #ChristchurchTerrorAttack. This img was shared by Nathan Sykes on his now closed blog. In it, Tom Sewell of The Lads Society states that the boys knew the killer and he'd been around since 2016. #antifa #auspol #FCKNZS #NewZealandMosqueAttack', 27 March 2019 <https://twitter.com/slackbastard/status/1110849967340425216>; see also Byron Kaye and Tom Allard, 'New Clues Emerge of Accused New Zealand Gunman Tarrant's Ties to Far Right Groups', Reuters, 4 April 2019.

1 'AN ACTUAL FASCIST'

1   Brenton Tarrant, 'The Great Replacement', 2019, p. 15.

2   See Richard J. Evans, 'Thank You, Dr Morell', *London Review of Books*, 21 February 2013, p. 37.

3   Ashley Hoffman, 'Godwin's Law: what the creator thinks of Hitler comparisons', *Time*, 29 June 2017.

4   Roger Griffin, *The Nature of Fascism* (Psychology Press, 1993), p. 26.

5   Umberto Eco, 'Ur-Fascism', *New York Review of Books*, 22 June 1995.

6   Robert O. Paxton, *The Anatomy of Fascism* (Alfred A. Knopf, 2004), p. 218.

7   Daniel Woodley, *Fascism and Political Theory: critical perspectives on fascist ideology* (New York: Routledge, 2009), p. 105.

8   Adolf Hitler, *Mein Kampf* <http://gutenberg.net.au/ebooks02/0200601.txt>.

9   Roger Eatwell, 'Political Violence and Institutional Crisis in Interwar Southern Europe', in *Rethinking the Nature of Fascism: comparative perspectives* (Palgrave Macmillan, 2010), p. 178.

10 Robert G.L. Waite, *Vanguard of Nazism: the free corps movement in postwar Germany, 1918–1923* (Harvard University Press, 1952), p. 42.

11 George L. Mosse, 'Introduction: The Genesis of Fascism', *Journal of Contemporary History*, 1.1 (1966), p. 17.

12 Tarrant, p. 34.

13 Tarrant, p. 73.

14 Martin Pugh, *'Hurrah for the Blackshirts'!: fascists and fascism in Britain between the wars* (Jonathan Cape, 2005), p. 120.

15 Nigel Jones, *Mosley: Life & Times* (Haus, 2004), p. 88.

16 Jones, p. 83.

17 Michael A. Spurr, '"Living the Blackshirt Life": culture, community and the British Union of Fascists, 1932–1940', *Contemporary European History*, 12.3 (2003), 305–22 (p. 311).

18 Jones, p. 102.

19 Pugh, p. 157.

20 Pugh, p. 286.

21 Richard C. Thurlow, 'The Guardian of the "Sacred Flame": the failed political resurrection of Sir Oswald Mosley after 1945', *Journal of Contemporary History*, 33.2 (1998), 241–54 (p. 250).

22 Stephen Dorril, *Blackshirt: Sir Oswald Mosley and British fascism* (Viking, 2006), p. 581.

23 Graham Macklin, *Very Deeply Dyed in Black: Sir Oswald Mosley and the resurrection of British fascism after 1945* (I.B. Tauris, 2007), p. 140.

2 'SWEEP IT ALL UP!'

1 Julian Borger, 'Blogger Bares Rumsfeld's Post 9/11 Orders', *The Guardian*, 24 February 2006.

2 Neta C Crawford, 'United States Budgetary Costs of the Post-9/11 Wars Through FY2019: $5.9 trillion spent and obligated' (Watson Institute International and Public Affairs, Brown University, 2018).

3 Douglas Little, *Us versus Them: the United States, radical Islam, and the rise of the green threat* (Chapel Hill: The University of North Carolina Press, 2016), p. 13.

4 Tarrant, p. 3.

5 Tarrant, p. 15.

6 Henry Ford, *The International Jew: the world's foremost problem* (CreateSpace Independent Publishing), p. 2.

7 David Noon, 'Happy Birthday, Mr. Ford. Love, Adolf', *The Chronicle of Higher Education*, 30 July 2008.

8 Edward W. Said, 'Orientalism Reconsidered', *Cultural Critique*, 1 (1985), 89–107 (p. 99).

9 Mattias Gardell, 'Terror in the Norwegian Woods', *Overland Literary Journal*, 2011, issue 205.

10 'Murdoch Says Muslims Must Be Held Responsible for France Terror Attacks', *The Guardian*, 10 January 2015.

11 Peter Hart, 'Bill O'Reilly Explains the "Muslim Problem"', FAIR, 20 May 2011; MPower Change, '86 Times Donald Trump Displayed or Promoted Islamophobia', *Medium*, 19 April 2018.

12 'K.K.K. Leader Admits Subsidizing Call for Boycott of Kosher Products', *Jewish Telegraphic Agency*, 17 February 1966.

13 Alex Mann, 'Why Are Some Australians Campaigning against Halal and What's Its Effect?', Australian Broadcasting Corporation, 20 November 2014.

14 Cory Bernardi, 'For Australia's Sake We Need to Ban the Burqa', *Sydney Morning Herald*, 6 May 2010.

15 Wajahat Ali and others, 'Fear, Inc.: the roots of the Islamophobia network in America', *Center for American Progress*, 26 August 2011 [accessed 25 April 2019].

16 Halima Kazem, 'Funding Fear of Muslims: $206m went to promoting "hatred", report finds', *The Guardian*, 20 June 2016.

17 Hamid Dabashi, 'Islamophobia, Liberal Zionism and Neoliberal Imperialism', *Alaraby*, 17 November 2014 [accessed 30 April 2019].

18 Matt Carr, 'You Are Now Entering Eurabia', *Race & Class*, 48 (1), 2006, p. 7.

19 Mark Steyn, *America Alone: the end of the world as we know it*, Regnery, 2006, p. xvi.

20 Michael Brull, '2,891 Murdoch Media Stories Trashing Islam In A Single Year, Study Reveals', *New Matilda*, 3 March 2018.

21 Tarrant, p. 3.

22 Thomas Chatterton Williams, 'The French Origins of "You Will Not Replace Us"', *New Yorker*, 27 November 2017.

23 David B. Green, 'This Day in Jewish History 1938: nations discuss jewish refugees, get nowhere, but then they hadn't planned to', *Haaretz*, 6 July 2015.

24 Hannah Arendt, *Imperialism: part two of the origins of totalitarianism* (Harvest, 1976), p. 149.

25 Williams.

26 Richard Spencer (ed), *The Great Erasure: the reconstruction of white identity*, Radix 1st edition (Washington Summit Publishers, 2012).

27 Michael Edison Hayden, 'New Zealand Terrorist Manifesto Influenced by Far-Right Online Ecosystem, Hatewatch Finds', Southern Poverty Law Center, 15 March 2019.

28 Alan Pyke, 'The Dark History of the New Zealand Killer's

"Great Replacement"', *Think Progress*, 15 March 2019.

29 Ted Hesson, 'Five Ways Immigration System Changed After 9/11', Australian Broadcasting Corporation News, 11 September 2012.

30 Sarah Gonzalez, 'No One Expected Obama Would Deport More People Than Any Other U.S. President', *WNYC*, 20 January 2017.

31 Marisa Franco and Carlos Garcia, 'The Deportation Machine Obama Built for President Trump', *The Nation*, 27 June 2016.

32 Aimé Césaire, *Discourse on Colonialism*, Translated by Joan Pinkham, (New York: MR, 1972), p. 35.

33 David A. Neiwert, *The Eliminationists: how hate talk radicalized the American right* (PoliPoint Press, 2009), p. 19.

34 Heather Digby Parton, 'Ann Coulter Has Fallen from Grace — and the Reason Why Is Terrifying', *Salon*, 29 June 2015.

35 David W. Moore, Gallup Inc, 'Bush Job Approval Highest in Gallup History', Gallup.com, 24 September 2001.

36 See Jeff Sparrow, *Trigger Warnings: political correctness and the rise of the right* (Scribe, 2018).

37 'Tea Party Canvass Results', *Washington Post*, 24 October 2010.

38 Nina Burleigh, 'Donald Trump and the FEMA Camps Crowd', *Newsweek*, 19 August 2016; Caitlin Dickson, 'Agenda 21: the UN conspiracy that just won't die', *Daily Beast*, 14 April 2014; Morgan Whitaker, 'Where Anti-Obama Fanatics Get Their "Facts"', MSNBC, 24 October 2013.

39 See Roger Eatwell and Matthew J. Goodwin, *National Populism: the revolt against liberal democracy* (Pelican, 2018), p. 57. Note, though, Eatwell and Goodwin do not see national populism as racist.

3 'HAIL TRUMP!'

1 Martin Pengelly, 'Word of the Year 2016: for Merriam-Webster, "surreal" trumps "fascism"', *The Guardian*, 19 December 2016.

2 BBC News, 31 August 2016.

3   M.J. Lee, 'Why Some Conservatives Say Donald Trump's Talk Is Fascist', CNN, 25 November 2015.

4   Max Ehrenfreund, 'Why You Should Stop Calling Donald Trump a Fascist', *Washington Post*, 4 December 2015; Jim Gilmore, 'Trump's Immigration Rhetoric Is "Fascist Talk"', *Buzzfeed News*, 21 November 2015.

5   Jamelle Bouie, 'Donald Trump Is a Fascist: it is the political label that best describes what the GOP front-runner has become', *Slate*, 25 November 2015.

6   Chokshi Niraj, 2016. 'Trump Accuses Clinton of Guiding Global Elite Against U.S. Working Class', *New York Times*, 13 October 2016.

7   Steve Guest, 'Trump: If A Protester Throws A Tomato At Me, "Knock The Crap Out Of Them"', *Daily Caller*, 1 February 2016.

8   Chauncey DeVega, 'Conservatism in the Age of Obama: Trump's violent rhetoric against Hillary has been festering for years within the GOP', *Salon*, 11 August 2016.

9   Joseph Goldstein, 'Alt-Right Gathering Exults in Trump Election With Nazi-Era Salute', *New York Times*, 20 November 2016.

10 David Greason, *I Was a Teenage Fascist*, (McPhee Gribble, 1994), p. 41.

11 Tarrant, p. 17.

12 T.K. Kim, 'Hate Website Stormfront Sees Rapid Growth of Neo-Nazi Community', Southern Poverty Law Center, 27 July 2015.

13 Eli Saslow, 'Hate Groups' Newest Target', *Washington Post*, 22 June 2008.

14 Andrew Jakubowicz, 'Alt_Right White Lite: trolling, hate speech and cyber racism on social media', *Cosmopolitan Civil Societies: an interdisciplinary journal*, 9.3 (2017), p. 41.

15 Dale Beran, '4chan: The Skeleton Key to the Rise of Trump', *Medium*, 14 February 2017.

16 Mattathias Schwartz, 'Malwebolence — The World of Web Trolling', *The New York Times*, 3 August 2008.

17 Richard Seymour, 'The Gamification of Fascism', *Patreon*, 29 April 2019.

18 Luke O'Brien, 'My Journey to the Center of the Alt-Right', *The Huffington Post*, 3 November 2016.

19 Ashley Feinberg, 'This Is The Daily Stormer's Playbook', *Huffington Post*, 14 December 2017.

20 O'Brien.

21 Ana Valens, '8chan Is at the Center of the Christchurch Mosque Shootings — and Its Roots Are in Gamergate', *The Daily Dot*, 15 March 2019.

22 Joshua Green, 'Inside the Secret, Strange Origins of Steve Bannon's Nationalist Fantasia', *Vanity Fair*, 17 July 2017.

23 Tina Nguyen, 'Far-Right Trump Adviser Tied to Anti-Semitic Paramilitary Group', *Vanity Fair*, 4 April 2017.

24 Spencer Sunshine, 'A Guide to Who's Coming to the Largest White Nationalist Rally in a Decade', Political Research Associates, 10 August 2017.

25 Jane Coaston, 'Trump's New Defense of His Charlottesville Comments Is Incredibly False', *Vox*, 26 April 2019.

26 Danny Katch, 'The Sad Spectacle of "Sloppy Steve" Bannon', *Truthout*, 14 January 2018.

27 Chris Schiano and Freddy Martinez, 'Neo-Nazi Hipsters Identity Evropa Exposed In Discord Chat Leak', *Unicorn Riot*, 6 March 2019.

28 Katie Mettler, 'How A Black Man "Outsmarted" Neo-Nazi Group — And Became Their New Leader', NDTV.com, March 2019.

29 Allie Contie, 'A Prominent American Hate Group Just Collapsed Because of an Affair', *Vice*, 15 March 2018.

30 Natasha Lennard, 'Is Antifa Counterproductive? White Nationalist Richard Spencer Would Beg to Differ', *The Intercept*, 17 March 2018.

31 Brett Barrouquere, 'Where Are They Now? Some of the Key Players in Unite the Right Have Faded from the Scene over the Last Year', Southern Poverty Law Center, 9 August 2018.

32 Susy Buchanan, 'Showdown in Shelbyville: how old school white nationalists failed to deliver in Tennessee', Southern Poverty Law Center, 31 October 2017.

33 Joshua Eaton, 'Hundreds of Anti-Racist Protesters Swarm

Tiny, Far-Right Rally in Boston', *Think Progress*, 18 August 2018.

4 'SCREW YOUR OPTICS!'

1 Taly Krupkin, Amir Tibon, and Judy Maltz, '"Screw Your Optics, I'm Going In": suspected white supremacist shooter behind Pittsburgh synagogue attack', *Haaretz*, 28 October 2018.
2 Jane Coaston, 'The Alt-Right Is Debating Whether to Try to Look Less Like Nazis', *Vox*, 10 August 2018.
3 Will Carless and Aaron Sankin, 'The Hate Report: the alt-right is a mess', *Reveal*, 23 March 2018.
4 Brendan O'Connor, 'The Fascist Right Is Bloodied and Soiled', *Splinter*, 29 March 2018.
5 Tarrant, p. 18.
6 Tarrant, p. 6.
7 Walter Laqueur, *The Age of Terrorism* (Little, Brown and Company, 1977), p. 54.
8 Robert Evans, 'Shitposting, Inspirational Terrorism, and the Christchurch Mosque Massacre', *Bellingcat*, 15 March 2019.
9 Tarrant, p. 47.
10 Talia Lavin, 'The Death of Fascist Irony', *New Republic*, 20 March 2019.
11 Paul E. Mullen, 'The Autogenic (Self-Generated) Massacre', *Behavioral Sciences and the Law*, 22, 2004.
12 Bonnie Berkowitz, Denise Lu, and Chris Alcantara, 'More Than 50 Years of U.S. Mass Shootings: the victims, sites, killers and weapons', *Washington Post*, 5 June 2019.
13 Mark Follman, Gavin Aronsen, and Deanna Pan, 'A Guide to Mass Shootings in America', *Mother Jones*, 31 May 2019.
14 Thomas G. Bowers, Eric S. Holmes, and Ashley Rhom, 'The Nature of Mass Murder and Autogenic Massacre', *Journal of Police and Criminal Psychology*, 25.2 (2010), 59–66 (p. 62).
15 Mark Ames, *Going Postal: rage, murder, and rebellion: from Reagan's workplaces to Clinton's Columbine and beyond* (Soft Skull Press, 2005), p.5.

16 Ames, p. 173.
17 William Broyles, Jr, 'Why Men Love War', *Esquire*, May 2014.
18 Broyles.
19 Jonathan Shay, *Achilles in Vietnam: combat trauma and the undoing of character* (Simon & Schuster, 1995), p. 84.
20 Hannah Arendt, 'Reflections on Violence', *New York Review of Books*, 27 February 1969.
21 Eric J. Leed, *No Man's Land: combat & identity in World War I* (Cambridge University Press, 1979), p. 41.
22 Brian E. Crim, 'Terror from the Right: revolutionary terrorism and the failure of the Weimar Republic', *Journal of Conflict Studies*, 27.2 (2007).
23 Dale Beran, '4chan: The Skeleton Key to the Rise of Trump', *Medium*, 15 February 2017.
24 ADL Center on Extremism, 'When Women Are the Enemy: the intersection of misogyny and white supremacy', Anti-Defamation League, July 2018.
25 'Elliot Rodger: how misogynist killer became "incel hero"', BBC, 26 April 2018.
26 Alex DiBranco, 'The Incel Rebellion', *Public Eye Magazine*, Spring 2018.
27 'Elliot Rodger: how misogynist killer became "incel hero"'.
28 Rick Anderson, '"Here I Am, 26, with No Friends, No Job, No Girlfriend": shooter's manifesto offers clues to 2015 Oregon college rampage', *Los Angeles Times*, 23 September 2017.
29 Harry Shukman, 'Online Comments Reveal Florida Gunman Nikolas Cruz Idolized Santa Barbara Shooter Elliot Rodger', *Babe*, 15 February 2018.
30 *Salvage* editorial board, 'Mass Media and the Theodicy of Terror — *Salvage* monthly editorial #2', *Patreon*, 19 March 2019.
31 O'Connor.
32 Weiyi Cai and Simone Landon, 'Attacks by White Extremists Are Growing. So Are Their Connections', *The New York Times*, 3 April 2019.
33 *Salvage* editorial board.
34 Charlie Warzel, 'Mass Shootings Have Become a Sickening Meme', *The New York Times*, 28 April 2019.

35 Tarrant, p. 15.
36 'The Territorial Solution to the Jewish Question', Holocaust. cz <https://www.holocaust.cz/en/history/final-solution/general-2/the-territorial-solution-to-the-jewish-question/> [accessed 9 June 2019].
37 John Earnest, 'Manifesto', 2019.
38 Warzel.
39 Robert Evans, 'Ignore The Poway Synagogue Shooter's Manifesto: Pay Attention To 8chan's /pol/ Board', *Bellingcat*, 28 April 2019.

5 'FORESTS, LAKES, MOUNTAINS, AND MEADOWS'

1 Tarrant, p. 15.
2 See, for instance, Stefan Molyneux's tweet: 'The NZ shooter hated Conservatism. He called himself an "eco-fascist." His favourite government was Communist China', <twitter.com/StefanMolyneux/status/1106418403177193472>, 14 March 2019.
3 Gaby Del Valle, 'When Environmentalism Meets Xenophobia', *The Nation*, 8 November 2018.
4 Richard Smyth, 'The Dark Side of Nature Writing', *New Humanist*, 20 June 2018.
5 Alexander Reid Ross, *Against the Fascist Creep* (AK Press, 2017), p. 25.
6 Tarrant, p. 38.
7 Sarah Manavis, 'Eco-Fascism: the ideology marrying environmentalism and white supremacy thriving online', *New Statesman*, 21 September 2018.
8 Robin MacKay and Armen Avanessian, #ACCELERATE# : the accelerationist reader (Urbanomic Media, 2014), p. 4.
9 Benjamin Noys, *Malign Velocities: accelerationism and capitalism* (Zero Books, 2014), p. x.
10 Matthew N. Lyons, 'The Christchurch Massacre and Fascist Revolutionary Politics', *threewayfight*, 18 April 2019.
11 Tarrant, p. 66.
12 F.T. Marinetti, 'The Futurist Manifesto' <http://bactra.org/T4PM/futurist-manifesto.html> [accessed 18 June 2019].

13 Quoted in Walter Benjamin, 'The Work of Art in the Age of Mechanical Reproduction' <https://www.marxists.org/reference/subject/philosophy/works/ge/benjamin.html> [accessed 18 June 2019].

14 Walter Benjamin.

15 Manavis.

16 Tarrant, p. 22.

17 Umair Haque, 'How Capitalism Torched the Planet and Left It a Smoking Fascist Greenhouse', *Eudaimonia and Co*, 10 October 2018.

18 Tarrant, p. 22.

19 Tarrant, p. 66.

6 'COBBERS'

1 Patrick Begley, 'Alleged Mosque Shooter's Meme Popular with Australian Far-Right Group', *Sydney Morning Herald*, 15 March 2019.

2 Alex Mann, Kevin Nguyen, and Katherine Gregory, '"Emperor Cottrell": Accused Christchurch Shooter Had Celebrated Rise of the Australian Far-Right', *ABC News*, 23 March 2019; Byron Kaye and Tom Allard, 'New Clues Emerge of Accused New Zealand Gunman Tarrant's Ties to Far Right Groups' Reuters, 4 April 2019.

3 Sasha Polakow-Suransky, 'How Europe's Far Right Fell In Love with Australia's Immigration Policy', *The Guardian*, 12 October 2017.

4 Alex Cullen, 'The Faces Behind the Reclaim Australia Movement', *Yahoo! News*, 18 October 2015.

5 Michael Safi, 'Reclaim Australia Rallies: protesters clash in Melbourne and Sydney', *The Guardian*, 4 April 2015.

6 'Who Are The Australian Defence League?', *New Matilda*, 29 January 2014.

7 'Far Right Targets Muslims with Hate Campaign', *New Zealand Herald*, 26 April 2014.

8 Andy Fleming, 'Reclaiming Reality', *Overland Literary Journal*, 23 April 2015; Danny Nalliah of Catch the Fire Ministries

discusses his relationship with the UPF in this Australian Broadcasting Corporation 'Background Briefing' piece: Christine El-Khoury, 'Anti-Muslim Extremists: how far will they go?', Australian Broadcasting Corporation Radio National, 22 November 2015.

9   Paul Toohey, 'Mind Wars: the extremists taking Australia to dark places', *Daily Telegraph*, 18 June 2016.

10 'No Jail for Melb Man for Racist Calls', SBS News, 12 February 2014.

11 Michael Bachelard and Luke McMahon, 'Blair Cottrell, Rising Anti-Islam Movement Leader, Wanted Hitler in the Classroom', *Sydney Morning Herald*, 16 October 2015.

12 See, for instance, 'Explaining Propaganda - YouTube' <https://www.youtube.com/watch?v=OYDSG36qhm4> [accessed 7 April 2019].

13 Julie Nathan, 'The Far Right, the "White Replacement" Myth and the "Race War" Brewing', Australian Broadcasting Corporation *Religion & Ethics*, 12 February 2019.

14 Juan Diego Quesada, 'New Zealand Mosque Shooting: New Zealand attacker had name of spanish killer on weapon', *El País*, 15 March 2019.

15 James Dowling, '"Anti-Islamist" Rally Organiser Shown Laughing at Death Footage', *Herald Sun*, 16 July 2015.

16 Nick Dyrenfurth, '"The Real Threat Facing Us"', *Australian Jewish News*, 24 August 2017.

17 Andy Fleming, 'Quotations from Chairman Blair Cottrell', *Slackbastard*, 27 July 2015.

18 Simon Thomsen, 'Sky News Just Put the Adam Giles Show in "Recess" over Blair Cottrell Interview', *Business Insider Australia*, 6 August 2018.

19 Richard Cooke, 'Age-Old Hate', *The Monthly*, July 2017.

20 Jakubowicz.

21 Jason Wilson, 'Australians Are Worried about Trump. But There's a Lot to Be Worried about at Home', *The Guardian*, 10 February 2017.

22 'Neil Erikson on Cottrell, Nazis & Nathan Sykes the Troll', *Vimeo*, <https://vimeo.com/298787115>

23 Mann, Nguyen, and Gregory.

24 Tarrant, p. 27.

25 Alex Mann, Kevin Nguyen, and Katherine Gregory, 'Christchurch Shooting Accused Brenton Tarrant Supports Australian Far-Right Figure Blair Cottrell', Australian Broadcasting Corporation, 23 March 2019.

26 Martin McKenzie-Murray, 'How Reclaim Australia Hid a "Terrorist"', *The Saturday Paper*, 13 August 2018.

27 Rachel Eddie and Jennifer Smith, 'United Patriots Front Leader Blair Cottrell Details Criminal History', *Daily Mail*, 13 June 2013.

28 Jessica Haynes and Anna Henderson, 'Sam Dastyari Warns White Nationalism on the Rise after Pub Ambush By Far-Right Group', Australian Broadcasting Corporation News, 9 November 2017; Anna Prytz and Noel Towell, 'Coffin-Bearing Far-Right Protesters Crash Moreland Council Meeting', *Age*, 12 October 2017; Josh Butler, 'White Nationalist Extremists Storm Gosford Church', *10 Daily*, 21 May 2018.

29 ablokeimet, 'UPF Nazis Menace Melbourne Anarchist Club', *Melbourne Anarchist Communist Group*, 1 November 2015 <Melbacg.wordpress.com/?s=UPF+Nazis+Menace>; Myriam Robin, 'Nationalist Group Invades 3CR Office, Uploads Dramatically Scored Video', *Crikey*, 9 November 2015.

30 Eddie and Smith.

31 Luke McMahon, 'Gun-Toting Anti-Muslim "crusader" at Lead of United Patriots Front', *Sydney Morning Herald*, 7 November 2015.

32 Louise Milligan, 'White Nationalists Found Guilty of Inciting Serious Contempt of Muslims', Australian Broadcasting Corporation, 5 September 2017.

33 Genevieve Gannon, 'Vic Man Loses Gun Permits over "Beheading"' *Yahoo! News*, 13 December 2016.

34 Imogen Richards, 'A Dialectical Approach to Online Propaganda: Australia's United Patriots Front, right-wing politics, and Islamic State', *Studies in Conflict & Terrorism*, Vol 42, No 1–2, 2019.

35 Andy Fleming, 'A Brief Guide To The Australian Far Right',

Slackbastard, 9 April 2019.

36 Willie Graf, 'Antipodean Resistance and the Lads Society', April 2019, *thewhiterosesociety*, <https://thewhiterosesociety. writeas.com/antipodean-resistance-and-the-lads-society> [accessed 20 June 2019].

37 Willie Graf.

38 Thomas Sewell, 'Leave Us Alone, or Else?', *Lads Society*, 2 May 2019.

39 Willie Graf.

40 Patrick Begley, 'Threats from White Extremist Group That "Tried to Recruit Tarrant"', *The Sydney Morning Herald*, 2 May 2019.

41 Tessa Akerman, 'Anti-Islam Activist Faces Trial', *Australian*, 6 February 2018.

42 Joanna Crothers, 'Melbourne's Trades Hall Targeted by Man Who Planned to Carry out Terrorist Attacks, Court Told', *Australian Broadcasting Corporation News*, 3 September 2018.

43 Rick Goodman, 'Accused Vic Extremist Was "Nuts": Witness', *The Standard*, 3 September 2018.

44 Crothers.

45 Australian Associated Press, 'Far-Right Terrorism Accused Phillip Galea Boasted of Plans, Court Told', *The Guardian*, 19 December 2016; Alex Mann, Kevin Nguyen, and Katherine Gregory, 'Christchurch Shooting Accused Brenton Tarrant Supports Australian Far-Right Figure Blair Cottrell', Australian Broadcasting Corporation, 23 March 2019.

46 McKenzie-Murray.

47 Andy Fleming, '#7SummerOfNazis: The True Blue Crew & Co. Go Hunting Blacks While Channel 7 Cheers', *Slackbastard*, 16 January 2018.

48 Joanna Menagh, '"My Mum's in Jail, My Dad's Dead and I Don't Know Why": 5yo Son of Neo-Nazi Murderer's Tragic Plea', Australian Broadcasting Corporation News, 8 May 2018.

49 Harriet Alexander, 'White Supremacist Michael Holt Sentenced to 4.5 Years for Weapons, Child Porn Offences', *Sydney Morning Herald*, 29 September 2017.

50 Rachel Olding, '"I'm Fully Prepared to Shoot Cops": messages

of white supremacist revealed', *Sydney Morning Herald*, 25 August 2017.

51 Andy Fleming, 'Antifa Notes: Reclaim Australia, Michael Holt, Richard Spencer', *Slackbastard*, 30 January 2017.

CONCLUSION

1 'Blair Cottrell', *YouTube* <https://www.youtube.com/channel/UC3GAof8xOgl5IwWrJaBKPng> [accessed 4 June 2019]; Hunter Wallace, 'New Zealand Mosque Mass Shooting', *Occidental Dissent*, 15 March 2019; Colin Liddell, 'Framing the Christchurch Horror', *Affirmative Right*, 16 March 2009.

2 Brett Barrouquere, 'After New Zealand Shooting, Far-Right, Racists Claim Victimhood, Hail Killer as Hero', Southern Poverty Law Center, 15 March 2019.

3 Travis LeBlanc, 'The Enigma of Christchurch', *Counter-Currents Publishing*, 2019 <https://www.counter-currents.com/2019/03/the-enigma-of-christchurch/> [accessed 4 June 2019].

4 Richard Seymour, 'The Gamification of Fascism', <https://www.patreon.com/posts/gamification-of-26416367> [accessed 6 June 2019].

5 Nick Duffy, '"Sick" Far-Right Video Game Lets People Play as Christchurch Mosque Shooter, Hitler and Trump', *iNews*, 2 June 2019.

6 No Notoriety <https://nonotoriety.com/> [accessed 9 June 2019].

7 Sean Mantesso, 'Jacinda Ardern's Ambitious Plan to End Online Extremism after the Christchurch Massacre', Australian Broadcasting Corporation News, 15 May 2019.

8 Jason Baumgartner, Fernando Bermejo, Emily Ndulue, Ethan Zuckerman, and Joan Donovan, 'What We Learned from Analyzing Thousands of Stories on the Christchurch Shooting', *Columbia Journalism Review*, 26 March 2019.

9 Denis Muller, 'Christchurch Attacks Provide a New Ethics Lesson for Professional Media', *The Conversation*, 20 March 2019.

10 'Hack Live: what happened when we debated Aussie patriotism', *Triple J*, 22 September 2016 ; Royce Kurmelovs and Rebecca Kamm, 'How the Alt-Right Trolled Triple J to Advance Their Agenda', Vice, 17 August 2017.

11 Amanda Meade, 'Outcry over Sky News Australia Interview with Far-Right Extremist', *Guardian*, 6 August 2018.

12 Fleming, '#7SummerOfNazis'.

13 Ian Bogost, 'The Meme Terrorists', *The Atlantic*, 30 April 2019.

14 Jack Shafer, 'Why New Zealand's Press Just Put on Blinders for Its Biggest Story', *Politico* <https://politi.co/2JgKjTB> [accessed 13 June 2019].

15 Andrew Bolt, 'The Foreign Invasion', *Daily Telegraph,* August 2018.

16 Bolt had earlier published multiple pieces praising Jean Raspail's racist novel *The Camp of the Saints*, a book Raspail had signed for him. See Andrew Bolt, 'French-Speaking, Raspail-Loving Handwriting Sleuth Wanted', *Herald Sun*, 15 August 2016.

17 Kevin Roose, 'The Making of a YouTube Radical', *The New York Times*, 8 June 2019.

18 Eshwar Chandrasekharan, 'You Can't Stay Here: the efficacy of Reddit's 2015 ban examined through hate speech', *Medium*, 19 September 2018; Rachel Kraus, 'Milo Yiannopoulos' Facebook Rant Shows That De-Platforming Actually Works', *Mashable*, 28 August 2018.

19 Nick R. Martin, 'Twitter Suspends Journalist for Book About the Far Right', *The Daily Beast*, 11 June 2019.

20 Elizabeth Dwoskin and Tony Romm, 'Facebook Purged over 800 U.S. Accounts and Pages for Pushing Political Spam', *Washington Post*, 11 October 2018.

21 Chris Hughes, 'It's Time to Break Up Facebook', *The New York Times*, 10 May 2019.

22 Mike Lillis, '"Unite the Right 2" Exposes White Nationalist Movement in Disarray', *The Hill*, 12 August 2018.

23 Kim Kelly, 'What the Media Gets Wrong About Antifa', *Medium*, 31 August 2018.

24 Reuters, 'Trump Hits His All-Time Low Approval Rating —

Same as After Charlottesville Violence', *Haaretz*, 23 April 2019.

25 Australian Associated Press, 'Scott Morrison Says He Wanted to "Address Fears on Islam, Not Exploit Them", in Tense Interview', SBS News, 22 March 2019.

26 David Renton, *The New Authoritarians* (Pluto Press, 2019), p. 232.

27 Zoë Schlanger, 'Climate Anxiety', *Quartz*, 30 May 2019.

28 Joe Sandler Clarke, 'Climate of Despair: how the state of our environment is affecting my mental health', *New Statesman*, 23 October 2018.

29 Michael Rosen, 'Fascism: I Sometimes Fear ...', Michael Rosen, 18 May 2014 <http://michaelrosenblog.blogspot. com/2014/05/fascism-i-sometimes-fear.html> [accessed 21 June 2019].

30 Naomi Klein, *This Changes Everything* (Penguin, 2014), p. 10.